JOHN CAIRNEY is well known to au
nationally through his one-man sh
many minds he is synonymous with
one of the leading interpreters of th

In more than 50 years as an arti,
recitalist, lecturer, director and theatre consultant. He is also a
published author and an exhibited painter. Trained at the Royal
Scottish Academy of Music and Drama, he was a notable Hamlet at
the Citizens' Theatre and a successful Macbeth at the Edinburgh
Festival. He was also *This Man Craig* on television and has appeared
in many films, including *Jason and the Argonauts* and *Cleopatra*.

Cairney gained a PhD from Victoria University in Wellington,
New Zealand, and has travelled internationally as a lecturer, writer
and consultant on Robert Louis Stevenson, Charles Rennie Mackintosh and Robert Burns. He has written books on each of these
famous Scots, as well as on football, theatre and his native Glasgow,
where he now lives with his New Zealand wife, actress and script-
writer, Alannah O'Sullivan.

For further information, see www.johncairney.com

By The Same Author

A Walk in the Park

*Exploring the Treasures
of Glasgow's Dear Green Places*

JOHN CAIRNEY

Luath Press Limited
EDINBURGH
www.luath.co.uk

First published 2016

ISBN: 978-1-910745-35-9

The paper used in this book is recyclable. It is made from
low chlorine pulps produced in a low energy, low emissions manner
from renewable forests.

Printed and bound by
Bell & Bain Ltd., Glasgow

Typeset in 10 point Sabon
by 3btype.com

To all park users everywhere who enjoy
a walk in the open.
To enjoy the fresh air or just wander
with their thoughts.

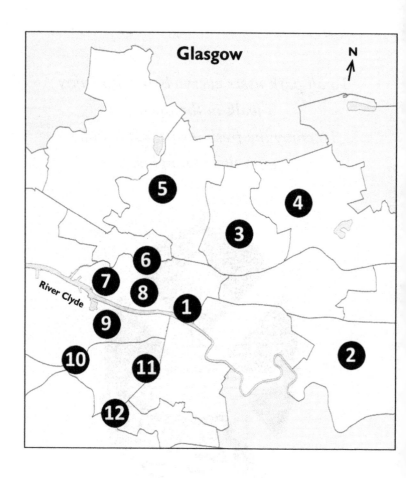

Contents

Contents

Ode to a Park

Any green space is a park to me
It's there to offer, for all to see.
All for free and a change of view
For city people just like you.
A park is not defined by its size
It's really a space built to surprise
By what's round the corner or over the hill
Beckoning and calling your feet, until
They can only respond by going
Along the path directed, knowing
It will lead to other pleasures.
Treasures of sight and sound
A riot of colour trimly bound
In beds of flowers, by bush and rock
And as you walk you can take stock
Of butterflies and begging squirrels
And rowdy children on roundabout whirls,
Notice courting couples wander
By the softer places yonder
Near the umbrella of sheltering trees
Where they may do as lovers please
Away from the crowd
In their own happy cloud
Safely held in the dance of romance
That's played in every park
From early day till falling dark.

The Parks

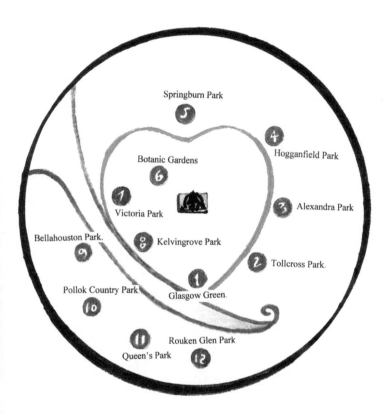

Springburn Park

5

4

Hogganfield Park

Botanic Gardens

6

7

Victoria Park

3

Alexandra Park

8

Kelvingrove Park

Bellahouston Park.

9

2

Tollcross Park.

1

Pollok Country Park.

10

Glasgow Green.

11

Rouken Glen Park

Queen's Park

12

Foreword

I'M FLATTERED and honoured to have been approached by John Cairney to write a foreword for his wonderful book celebrating our city's parks. I'm sure it will appeal to a wide audience for it is not simply about Glasgow's well-loved green places. It also explores what it means to be a Glaswegian, our city's rich history and the huge sense of pride our citizens share.

From small beginnings, Glasgow grew from a small rural settlement on the River Clyde to become the largest seaport in Britain. Its journey from a humble, medieval bishopric and royal burgh, to a major centre of the Scottish Enlightenment in the 18th century is well documented. It was the Clyde, the lifeblood of this city, that helped Glasgow make its fortune as one of Great Britain's main hubs of transatlantic trade with North America and the West Indies.

The ushering in of the Industrial Revolution saw an explosion in the city's population, size and economy. This earnt it a reputation as one of the world's pre-eminent centres for chemicals, textiles and engineering, most notably in the shipbuilding and marine engineering industry, which produced many innovative and famous vessels. Throughout the Victorian era, Glasgow's status as an industrial and commercial powerhouse led to it being referred to as 'The Second City of the Empire'.

'People Make Glasgow' is our latest marketing slogan and it's proved immensely successful. Quite simply it resonates across the globe for it recognises that it is our people, above all, who have made our city great. The people, across history, helped build Glasgow and its reputation as the friendly city.

As a proud Glaswegian, I'm also able to confirm that Glaswegians possess a fierce sense of justice and fairness and have an unfailing ability to see humour in adversity. These quintessential qualities have made them resilient. They truly are this city's greatest asset. They have allowed it to reinvent itself and flourish into the modern, exciting vibrant, multicultural and welcoming city it is today.

Glasgow is also a city that has had a clutch of accolades bestowed upon it including: European City of Culture; City of Architecture and Design; City of Science and UNESCO City of Music. I'm sure you'll agree there is a lot to recommend it.

It would be remiss of me, in light of the author's talents, not to acknowledge that this is also a city that has a reputation for artistic endeavour. Glasgow, as well as being home to art galleries and museums with world-class collections, is also a magnet for the creative arts. Scottish Ballet, Glasgow School of Art, the Royal Conservatoire, BBC and STV have all made their home here.

We are also fortunate to belong to a city of great natural beauty. Our parks are hugely valued by everyone. They are the essence of Glasgow – our dear green place. I trust this book will entertain and inform you about our parks, this city and its people.

Sadie Docherty, Lord Provost of Glasgow

Preamble

I HAVE TO STATE quite clearly at the outset that this is NOT a
guidebook to Glasgow. I prefer to think of it as a series of 12 short
essays by a native 'weegie' unashamed to trumpet his love of the
place and pleased by the chance to offer, in his modest volume, a
considered tribute to one of his city's lesser-known assets – its parks.
These essays contain comment, historical information, ideas and
anecdotes as they arise during the author's perambulations. These
cultivated areas within the extensive urban span are an increasingly
important element in the attempt to meet the environmental needs
of a future generation and continuing work on them is therefore
vital and to be encouraged. They are the initial factors that
inspired the book in the first place and the stimulations received
in the walks gave the pages their content. What struck me right
away, that the park, wherever it was situated, was a living thing.
But then, that depends on how one defines life.

> *Life is in the slip of a smile on the Mona Lisa's face*
> *The first notes of a nightingale in the forest,*
> *And in the gathering of clouds around a new moon*
> *And in the love between people,*
> *Which makes living almost worshipful*

Parks are not perhaps the first thing that one associates with Glasgow, so it may come as a surprise to learn that there are more of
them in my home city than in any other city of equivalent size in
Britain. There are no less than 90 officially listed green spaces
within the city and there would be even more were the list to
reach out and include public land available in fertile areas within
the Greater Glasgow borders that mark the old Strathclyde.

The truth is that Glasgow is green and getting greener every
day. Behind the traditional tenements, beyond the towering glass
and concrete office boxes, beside the ubiquitous motorways and
underneath the railway bridges you will find the inevitable greenery.
Some city parks are the size of a regular garden and others of a
small county. We have them all sizes in Glasgow. It is this alloca-

tion of green per head of population that makes the city literally, as well as historically, a 'dear green place'.

Another fact, borne out by Joe Fisher's *Glasgow Encyclopedia*, is that Glasgow's parks are something of a horticultural phenomenon. Not just for their hectares of green grass, or the sheer number of trees to be seen, but also for their stupendous floral spread. Comparisons with respective acreages tells us there are more flowers in any single Glasgow park than there are in the whole city of Paris!

Mais oui, c'est vrai!

Interestingly, it was a French author, Montesquieu, who pointed out that the character of any nation is defined by its climate. It is ironic therefore, that even now in Paris, 195 countries are meeting in an attempt to arrive at a global deal that will tackle the growing problem of climate change. They are discussing plans for a worldwide reduction of greenhouse gas emissions to zero in the next half century. Hopefully the agreed upon terms will include loans to poorer countries and will assist them in making regular reports about emission-cutting targets. The goal is to limit global temperature rise, and at the same time reduce carbon emissions worldwide. Unfortunately, everyone has to agree on what action has to be taken and international solidarity is difficult to achieve on any subject. In this respect, mankind has always been its own worst enemy. In ancient days it was the strong in physique who won the day, then as we became more sophisticated it was the strong in guile. Soon we were divided into rich and poor, black and white, large and small, the educated minority or the uneducated, any demarcation would do as long as it lent power, however temporary, and gave justification to any wilful, gainful act.

So the centuries rolled on and crushed the greater good in the interests of the greedy few who manipulated the many, whatever cult or fashion was in vogue. There have always been divisions and differences down the long trail of history and we, in our time, are little changed. If there was no battle brewing an excuse would be found to start one because the basic aim was power. Power meant territory and territory meant money.

And now Nature itself appears to have joined the conspiracy against the common good. Today we have strong winds that

A WALK IN THE PARK

nearly blow you off your feet and heavy rainstorms, the weight and force of which have not been seen in Britain for years. Recently rivers flooded their banks to such an extent that motorways were closed, railway lines washed out and thousands of homes flooded throughout the north of England and southern Scotland. It's as if somebody or something is angry with humanity and is trying to tell us something. We'd better listen and listen well, before it's too late. Appreciation of nature and what we may be irreparably damaging is surely as essential as international conferences?

We must find our way back to Mother Nature again. And where better to start than the park, or at least its equivalent open space. To walk is to talk with your body; to adjust every muscle movement to the strict rhythm of your own heart beat. And like anything done with the heart, it can only come out well, despite any doubts we might have about our legs. As the saying goes, 'It is the heart that makes the man.'

Introduction

Oh, Beautiful City of Glasgow,
That stands on the River Clyde,
How happy must the people be
That in you reside.
You are the greatest city of the present day
Whatever anybody else might say!

WILLIAM McGONAGALL

THIS SNATCH OF McGonagall may not be high poetry but it is right on the mark as an indication of Glasgow's status in 2016. The city enjoyed a specially designated Green Year in 2015 and it was this fact alone that prompted this book. There is certainly, in the place, at the time of writing, a determined undertaking by the City Council to draw public attention to a hitherto underrated municipal asset, its many public parks.

To walk in a park is something we decide to do, not just the confirmed dog walkers, joggers, health enthusiasts, etc, but ordinary pedestrians who just like to walk, an act most of us elect to do without thinking. We just throw one foot out and the other follows – but every walk, no matter where, over street, roadway, mountain track or park, is different because it's in another place at another time. My father used to tell me that any walk is only from here to there. It's just as far as you can see. He said it was no use worrying about what was around the corner or over the hill, you need to get to where you can see it for yourself; to anticipate troubles is not productive, it only adds to the anxieties that might lie ahead.

Any trip calls for sensible planning and the accepting of any hazards encountered. We deal with its stages as they happen, that way we miss nothing. There is no feeling like the footfall. It is a natural act that allows the other senses to kick in. You can look up and around as you will, without the restrictions of driving or navigating public transport. You can sing, or talk to a friend – or to yourself, there is no better friend after all. There is no need to hurry or worry while walking – we do that in life all the time. When we walk we can just give in to the moment.

Conversely, perhaps the best thing about park walking is that we don't have to talk to anyone at all if we don't want to. A walk is a rare chance to enjoy some healthy musing and reap the medicinal benefits of silence. With the calm it allows we can react immediately to whatever the body is trying to tell us. But the point is, we have to listen. When young Chopin was ill in Warsaw, he was told to walk as much possible. Could it be he picked his wonderful melodies out of the Polish air as he did so?

In our own day, Chris McCulloch Young organised an outdoor event entitled, Walk a Mile in My Shoes on the same Chopin principal, that a walk can do you nothing but good. The McCulloch principle is to walk *with* someone for a mile, talking as you go, for at least a half an hour. This gives an opportunity to share the experience with a stranger, who will not remain a stranger for long as you step out; two friends will finish the exercise. No training is needed, no qualifications, just pick a pal and a park and get started. This is easily done in Glasgow, for as Mr McCulloch says, 'You walk into Glasgow and it's a city that thinks it a village, everyone wants to talk to you and hear your stories and tell you theirs.'

This is easy in a park, especially in a Glasgow park. Let the last word be with Chris McCulloch: 'On the Walk in the Green... everyone is on a level playing-field. It's about breaking down barriers and seeing how fabulous people are.'

Glasgow couldn't agree more as witness its current municipal slogan – People Make Glasgow.

Alone, out with only the wind around us and with no responsibilities, other than to keeping moving, we can respond to feelings. We react to the emotions green spaces arouse and to all we see or hear around us while in them. Anything goes on a walk, particularly a walk in the park. Although a walk anywhere is healthful, it is particularly so in a park. All parks are man-made, but from a natural source. They are formed primarily to provide the ultimate freedom – to breathe in and step out, to enjoy the walk and feel the better for it. Park space was, and still is for many Glasgow citizens, a vital ingredient of their necessary escape grid second only to the cinema.

Each of the city's green resorts, in its different way, fed hungry minds at their most inquiring, and people also ate up what the parks had to offer scenically, especially in their own local districts. Parks were once the prime recourse in hard times because they were the cheapest, the most available and the least demanding. A visit to the park was just a matter of walking. And what could be a simpler action? After all, feet were made for walking. And they do just that in numbers in Glasgow, whatever the weather. The ground below may be summer green, autumn brown or winter grey, but the Glaswegian gets out there.

The truth is, it is the citizen element, the human environmental, which really makes any conurbation the living place it is, whatever its geographical location. Glasgow itself is on the same latitude as Moscow. However, it is set right at the edge of north-west Europe, and, until recently at least, it was favoured by westerly Atlantic winds and it is sheltered by hills to the north, the east and the south. This means that temperatures have long been constant, never too warm in summer or unbearably cold in winters – although admittedly the city has its quasi-arctic winter moments with snow, and rain is always a problem.

What I found incredible in personally researching these parks was that the land that was to become my land was once part of an immense forest in a country that was first called Caledonia by the invading Romans before it become Scotland. Originally it lay on a coastal plain on the edge of a shallow sea just above the Equator. In that far-distant geological phase the landmass was unattached to England and boasted a tropical climate. However, even then great changes threatened, and very gradually came about. The earth moved, rivers brought down sand and mud, the rains came, great hurricanes blew, and what is now central Scotland was moved to the north west, up to the very rim of Europe where it has remained ever since, stuck to England, a hand-reach away from Ireland and a decent swim away from France.

In comparison with this primeval activity, the initial emergence of parks in Scotland is a recent phenomenon. In the first decades of the 19th century Glasgow was a thriving trading centre, rich in profits from the export of African peoples to America and the return import of cotton for factories all over Britain, she was riding high in the market-place. The Glasgow merchant was right up there with the times, and so the Merchant City was developed in Glasgow city centre as an integral part of this municipal success. Huge profits were made and lost but funds were suddenly made available to city leaders and park development was only one of the many projects initiated. This is the kind of public spirited action that typifies the city today, even as it goes forward in its modern surge towards a new identity.

This optimistic attitude is typified by the drive to 'go green' and create even more leisure spaces for the public good. This move towards environmental responsibility and the continuing focus on common space is the sort of thing that is giving a Glasgow a good name at the moment. The name itself 'Glasgow' (never Glas-COW as I've heard it called around the world!) comes from a Celtic/Pictish/Gaelic amalgam meaning 'green', which is why it has long been known as The Dear Green Place. Green is currently fashionable. It is good for everything, for health, for appearance and for growth, and Glasgow certainly has grown considering how inauspicious its beginnings were. These beginnings were frugal to say the least, but have won the fight to rise in its own way, even if on some days the old bruises show. The city's development over nearly 900 years is indeed remarkable. It began with a cathedral, soon had a university and then had its market-place; all the ingredients that make any city. The only difference is that Scotland's largest city was entirely self-made. No matter what changes occur – political, material or climatic – Glasgow will always be Glasgow. Despite its persistent rough and ready image, and all the accruing clichés and misrepresentations that have clung to its image over the years, it will never let a good thing go to waste.

Glasgow still has the honour of creating the first ever space allocated to the common people for their grazing animals or leisure use. This fundamental event occurred in 1450, when Bishop Turnbull gifted the area of land by the river which was to become Glasgow Green, the first-ever park or green space for leisure and recreation in Britain. The very much later Victorian municipal parks system which was to grow out of this area was originally devised by James Cleland, the City Statistician and Superintendent of Public Works, in 1813.

Steps towards the parks system had already been taken as early as the mid-18th century, but the serious work was carried out by the Victorians around 1813 and their mark is still visible to this day. Glasgow Green was extensively extended in the course of the next century by succeeding Park Superintendents like James Weston and Duncan McLellan who confirmed the parks as a unique recreational and cultural asset to latter-day Glasgow. It is to men like these that Glasgow owes its impressive park heritage. A heritage that led Glasgow ultimately to become originator of its own Garden Festival in 1988, the European City of Culture in 1990, host of the World Orchid Show in 1993, the City Parks Conference of 1994 and also a setting for the World Rose Convention in 2007. All this park work still goes on, as the new Peace Garden development adjacent to the Tramway Art Gallery and Performance Area in Albert Drive, not far from the home of Scottish Ballet in Pollokshaws Road, now shows. And, by the way, the city was also named European City of Architecture in 1999. Not bad for a place that's still only associated in many minds with working boots, booze and bunnets!

Life in Glasgow today is, for true Glaswegians at least, centred on conversation. The chat or the patter, as they call it, is a way of life for many – pithy, realistic and to the point, talk is the thing. Never waste words but never abuse them either, unless you're trying to get a laugh of course. And life's a laugh, or at least you've got to make it seem so. Wherever one goes in Glasgow, whoever one meets, even in a park, there's always a laugh in it. Humour is the first resort in any situation for any Glaswegian, their first survival weapon.

Behind the ready tongue, however, is a big heart. Any visitor to the city will understand this very quickly, for the citizens of the place will come to him or her without inhibition and with complete ease. Glasgow doesn't believe in strangers; the Glaswegian sees everyone as a pal first, and one has to earn the right to be an enemy. That's why the Glasgow native will talk to anybody. I know that to define a person merely by their location is often to denigrate them, but there is no doubt that the born and raised Glaswegian has a particular aura that is unique. It is compounded largely of irreverence and yet, beneath it all is a basic kindness and quite unexpected warmth and generosity.

Not everyone, however, loves Glasgow. Eugen D'Albert, a noted early 20th-century composer and pianist, was born in the city when his father was working in Glasgow as a music teacher. Eugene made no secret of his dislike of the place and as soon as he could he returned to Germany, where he enjoyed a busy musical career and made something of a career out of marriage, too – as he got hitched six times! The late Dirk Bogarde, of British film fame, told me personally how much he loathed Glasgow while he was at Alan Glen's school as a boy. He was only there because his mother was a Glaswegian, and insisted that he, like her, should be educated in Glasgow. Dirk escaped to the army just before the end of the Second World War, and he never could understand what anybody saw in his mother's birthplace. In short, Glasgow, however atypical its historical image, is today a bustling, thriving, forward-looking metropolitan hub.

Today's world is obsessed by differences – whether it's in language or colour or religious belief. Difference appears to be an essential element in defining not only nationality but personal identity, forgetting that we are all basically identical under the skin no matter the variety of shields we proffer. Nowhere can this be better seen when people are away from their own environment and comfortable associations. Even in a park, away from their known ties and comforting familiarities and out in the open in the fresh air, Glaswegians tend to 'perform' – but not for long.

The public park is the place where your most basic identity is thrust upon you. The visitor is open to its effects, fresh air, colour and freedom from the normal restrictions. There are few locked doors in a park, there are no curtains to close discreetly, no blinds to pull down. You get what you can see, whether it's a good view or a coffee in the garden centre. Parks are no longer open from dawn to dusk as they once were. Many are now open at all times to all comers. I am told by those in charge of such things that it's a matter of costs, particularly in the payment of wardens, park keepers and rangers. The positive effect is that parks are there for anyone as long as they can see where they are going. The basic thing to remember may be that when walking in the open, the best view you might get in the end is of yourself. A park is a total parallel of life in that you find your path, if you're lucky. We are lucky to have so many in our beautiful, ever changing city.

How then, in less than a thousand years, did Glasgow develop into the city full of parks it is today? We must first consider its motto 'Let Glasgow Flourish'. It originally ended with 'by the preaching of the Word and the Praising of his Name'. In other words, the city had a totally religious foundation. However, Glasgow is now centuries away from its missionary beginnings. It is, nevertheless, a fact that its beginnings were holy. This is specifically due to a young monk with aristocratic blood, St Kentigern, better known by his later pet name, Mungo, who travelled across southern Scotland from Fife seeking a burial place for his church mentor, Fergus. (The story is dealt with more fully in chapter 5).

Metaphorically, if we liken Glasgow's growth to our own accepted seven ages we see that its infancy was indeed church-led and its early development entirely missionary. Its later childhood was rural and lightly agricultural, developing into riparian village activities as early commercial industries, like mills, took advantage of its riverside location. The city's proximity to the sea endowed it with its later port possibilities and led to the immense profits made in the 18th century from the slave and tobacco trades in what could be called Glasgow's youth. Its early manhood was celebrated by the building of homes and businesses, eventually tenements and factories, and the cultivation of land as commercial property. The weavers arrived in Glasgow's middle age which bloomed as railways took over from shipping and led later to heavy armaments for the Great War of 1914 and to even higher profits. Then followed something of a dip as the Depression years between the two World Wars coincided with what could be termed as Glasgow's old age, which was ironically saved only by the war of 1939. Bullets and shells can always be relied upon to boost the economy.

The present day boom in Glasgow is, without doubt, a second childhood of pop culture, the arts and a clutch of Turner Prize winners. And all this was very much against the odds. The plain truth, and one which should be have been guessed, is that under the clichéd cloth cap there are brains, the blistered hands are nimble, the feet in the working boots can dance, and the abrasive voice can sing. The slightest acquaintance with Glasgow shows this, just as any walk in its parks might do. It is no misnomer to think of a park as an open space. You can only be 'in the open' while you're there. Perhaps the openness is the effect of the wind in your face. It certainly gets rid of the cobwebs.

Every park is its own unique place and there is a basic bond between local people and these places – who doesn't remember their childhood home? Or some other special place in the past that spoke clearly to them? We must always bear in mind that whoever we are, wherever we live, at root, it's the same for all of us, this business of being temporarily in the world. We have to cherish our roots whatever they are, and where better to look for roots than in a park?

On a wider front, we can even consider Scotland's social evolution in terms of land use. Current criminal investigations arising from the scandal caused by the bribery and corruption discovered at FIFA, the headquarters of world football, bring to mind the subtle operation by the Scottish upper classes over the last 300 years to obtain and retain land and property in Scotland. This was a similar use of elected power for profit, land use, or rather its ownership, has always been a Scottish problem. Property value in land tax alone might have paid for Glasgow's highly-successful 2014 Commonwealth Games, but the grabbing and keeping of landed property was a sport from which the ordinary people were (and largely still are) totally excluded.

To compound this issue, the same ordinary people were once the common owners of the land they occupied and their clan chiefs were the elders, elected to advise and govern. Soon, the chieftainship became a family matter, and superior peerage was accepted, heritage was established and class was born. Those who had land kept it and those who did not went without. Division was rife and strictly held to at the higher levels. True democracy was merely a dream. Glasgow merchants, on the other hand – the entrepreneurs, like the Glassfords, the Grahams, the Millers and the Bogles – had made their fortunes in the early United States by daring invention and risk with tobacco, cotton and later black slaves. But they gave back much of what they made to their own city by building beautiful houses for themselves and erecting splendid offices in the city centre, many of which still stand, giving the City of Glasgow, a superbly designed inner core.

This inner-city architecture is only another of Glasgow's under-rated treasures. Yet even these buildings are at a remove from the common people, who are still now, as when the buildings were first erected, vulnerable to the whims of self-appointed money lords and property masters. A minority ruling class has been upheld for centuries thanks to a carefully-wrought legal system that only sees their point of view. The few still have complete control over the many. Today, 432 people own half of the available land in Scotland. Too few own too much, as Andy Wightman has tried to tell us in his excellent book, *The Poor had no Lawyers*. Despite recent moves towards some land reform, it may need more than the current Scottish National revival to restore Scotland to its sturdy and independent Scottish selfhood. Today it would seem merely a matter of wardrobe. Chinless, kilted figures posing for photographs hardly defines our racial dignity and scenic sentimentality. They may be good for postcards and tourist brochures but they should be confined to that kind of out-dated nationalism. A new kind of reformation may be called for.

There is no doubt that Scotland has diminished nationally since the hurried 1707 Union and 'Britain' is still referred to as 'England' by most of the world, where, oddly enough, an old Scottish pride is still maintained by the Scottish diaspora who have emigrated to Canada, the United States, South Africa, South America, Hong Kong, Australia and New Zealand and to almost everywhere else world-wide. It is a truism that wherever you find banks, football or golf, you can be assured the Scots have been. And who gave the idea of the National Park to America? A Scot, of course, the bearded John Muir from Dunbar. As a direct result, the United States has a magnificent ring of parks today. Sites like Yosemite and Death Valley attract tourists by the millions every year, and everyone wants to walk in Arizona's Grand Canyon.

In Scotland we may not have such epic ground spaces but those of us who are still native to our own piece of the world have to live with what we've got in Glasgow, which should be more than enough for anyone. The *status quo* is sufficient and our only reassurance might be that we still have our national pride and we still, as a community, own all our parklands. This was ratified by the Select Committee on Public Walks set up in 1833 and confirmed by the Recreation Grounds Act of 1859, with the result that *Spencer's English Traveller* in 1871 called Glasgow 'the most handsome city in Scotland'.

In Victorian times, the initial rush of weavers were the first to put these acres to recreational use after they helped create them. The Irish incomers followed suit after their potato famine forced them into lives abroad and they found relief and escape in the park from the over-crowded slum closes and wynds hurriedly built up to accommodate them.

In our own day, with the sheer number of parks, golf courses, bowling greens, putting greens and children's play spaces in Green Glasgow it is hard to believe that its parks are indeed the city's best-kept secret, but there is at least some relief in knowing that it's in them ordinary people can enjoy the pleasures of what is still their common land. The public park is the green symbol of basic democracy and long may it remain so.

As its motto maintains, Glasgow has flourished, but it also thrived by the planting of the seed and the raising of the plant. The seed fell in most unlikely ground, but the plants flowered eventually. Daniel Defoe confirmed this when writing of Glasgow in his *Tour Through the Island of Great Britain* between 1724 and 1726. He described Glasgow thus:

'In a word, 'tis one of the cleanest, most beautiful and best-built cities in Great Britain.'

It is a pleasant surprise to note how many English citizens like Glasgow. My own experience among fellow actors confirms this and a big surprise is that its theme song, 'I Belong to Glasgow' was written by an Englishman for Will Fyffe, a Dundonian, to sing. But then everything about the place, even today, is a surprise. That is one of its principal attractions. For instance, there is a modern office building in Parkhead, my own home district, entirely devoted to the study and use of natural energy. This is one resource that has never been in short supply in Glasgow. Indeed, it could be said that contemporary Glasgow is the energy centre for arts and culture in Scotland as is verified by attendances at each of the new performing arenas built along the riverside which attract thousands.

Yet all this new status confirmation with its attendant hysteria sprang from a simple medieval religious enthusiasm which can still be seen yet in nearly 150 of the city's street names and places. It sometimes seems that there are more spires in Glasgow than in Oxford. These indicate the vast numbers of churches, chapels and religious centres in the city, most of them with saints' names drawn from the horde of holy men who swarmed to join Kentigern around the Molendinar Burn.

Unfortunately, this former splashing stream, a vital element in the Glasgow story, a spiritual as well as a geographical link, is now culverted along most of its length and exists today as little more than an underground sewer. What a real treasure it might be for Glasgow if this potentially valuable water resource were opened up as an amenity at points in the city – especially in the north at Royston Park. It could also act as a flood preventative, and help to avoid incidents like the flooding of the Camlachie Burn in 2001. The Molendinar is moving yet under our feet. It should be utilised. It belongs to our city's beginning and therefore is a continuing emblem of our vigorous past.

The late Jack House, a Glaswegian *par exellence*, and winner of the St Mungo Prize in his day, thought the same and suggested in his *Evening Citizen* column that the Molendinar could become again the limpid stream it once was. It could rejoin the Gulf Stream off Ireland and make its way across the Atlantic down past the Falkland Islands round the Horn and out into the rest of the world making our wee trickle of water truly international. But, he insisted, it would still belong to Glasgow. And Glasgow likes what's hers.

Glasgow Green

1450 · 136 acres

Walk with me, oh my Lord,
Through the darkest night and brightest day.
Be at my side, oh Lord
Hold my hand and guide me on my way...

'WALK WITH ME OH LORD'

IT SEEMS APPROPRIATE to begin these park walks with a snatch of hymn, because Glasgow itself had a religious start, as we shall discover, and the very first park here was the idea of a Bishop at the time. However, Glasgow Green, as we know it now, is more than a park, it's Glasgow's mother-park, a badge of municipal pride and an emblem of civic attainment. More than that, it is a banner of a unique heritage, an earthy flag laid out over its tidy 136 acres to tell the world that it is not only Glasgow's first park, but its oldest and inarguably, its most famous for a whole manner of historical associations, the latest being the 2014 Commonwealth Games. For this event, virtually the whole of the East End suddenly underwent a positive revolution in housing with the provision of new amenities by which a former industrial area found a whole new attractiveness.

The effect of this widespread overhaul was, frankly, overwhelming. I am not saying so merely as a native of the area concerned, although I do realise that were I to look out of my former tenement bedroom today I would not recognise the tree-lined boulevard and gardens that my old Williamson Street has now become. Where I once saw factory sheds and smoke-grey tenements is now a spruce, and very desirable, place to live. A middle-class stamp has been imposed on a traditional working-class area and this has taken everyone by surprise, not least the surviving locals. There is definitely a growing awareness of new values in the East End, especially among the older residents who now see trees where once there were lamp-posts and coffee places that used to be pubs, but one thing remains exactly as it was, and that is the old Green – yes, the park they call Glasgow Green.

The finely laid stones of what was once Jocelyn Square are still there at the park's front gate, laid out as an imposing space now ringed with trees. What catches the attention in the Saltmarket behind are the magnificent Judiciary Buildings and Courthouses on the right but the Glaswegian tends to avert the eyes when in the vicinity of police structures despite a very pleasant view given of the Albert Bridge as it crosses over the Clyde to the Gorbals, and of my old haunt, the Citizens' Theatre. It was also here in the Square, facing the park, that from 1814, Glasgow's convicted murderers were hanged before crowds of thousands until the final offender, Dr Pritchard, met his end in 1865.

The Green goes a long way back and I had a slight feeling of awe about it, but, taking a deep breath, and humming one of my father's old pipe tunes, I marched bravely through the arch and on to the broad avenue that led me into 'Green land'. It's hard to realise that this manicured expanse was once a swamp taken over by the early church as a resource for the common people nearly twenty centuries ago. Would they have looked on the same sky as I do now, I wondered, or felt the same sun in their eyes, the same wind at their backs? It was a solemn thought

Glasgow Green began as a potential park in 1150 when Bishop Turnbull donated the patch of turf, from lands given him by King James II, as common grazing land for the benefit of the poor. It wasn't the most prepossessing of gifts. The whole area was flat, an ugly, empty yellow-brown stretch of earth between two small villages, Calton and Bridgeton, where the common people grazed their cows on what little grass there was and hung out their skimpy washing on any space that was available. It was land that amounted to little more than a filthy swamp but it belonged entirely to the ordinary people and they made full use of it in every way possible. To be honest, this first park was hardly a park to start with, more a practical, domestic utility put to good use by an underprivileged community. Similar patches of acreage were available for common use further east in Camlachie, to the north in Springburn, to the west at Partick and on the southern bank of the Clyde.

My concern, however, was for the turf I was treading so I kept moving just as Glasgow has kept moving since the moment it started. I am happy to take what comes my way as I walk on. That's the thrill of it, that's the adventure. The same might be said of East End parks today except that one is unlikely to see washing hanging out, although cattle and even sheep have returned to some parks as I would later discover. The fact was that all these ground spaces were to serve as the basis for the later municipal parks system which was to make its real start seven centuries later. This additional amenity grew to become a significant feature of the city in the following hundred years and confirm Glasgow's place as a unique recreational hub. And it all began here where I was walking.

There are more than a score of first-rate parks of size inside Glasgow today and their splendid condition is a tribute to not only the many previous City Councils' far-sightedness and courage but to the citizens' pride in what was created on their behalf. Glasgow Green's history records other, older times when ordinary people had a place in the nation and that place was territorial. It was completely theirs, in every sense, even though it was less than second-rate land. This ownership by the common people was rare, but it was welcomed.

'Go for the flagpole!' That's was the first thing I was told by an experienced park-walker. 'It tells you everything,' he said. I thanked him and promised to look for the flagpole. 'And another thing,' he added.

'Yes?'

'You'll never see a flag on it.'

'Oh?'

That was odd. What else was a flagpole for? After all, generations of men have followed their particular flag since nations first emerged. It must mean something, even if it's only a basic announcement of allegiance to whoever or whatever. Since the pole goes high it's meant to be seen, so why not a Glasgow coat of Arms on every pole? It might encourage a feeling of being above petty concerns and reach us up to higher considerations. But then people rarely look up. It's straight ahead or nothing. Maybe so, but whatever it may mean, the flagpole is at least a starting point and here I was standing under one in Glasgow Green. My walker friend was right, there was no flag.

What there *was*, however, were trees. So many tiny trees of equal size and foliage lining the main pathway from the park entrance that it was almost daunting. I noticed them as soon as

I had gone through the McLennan Arch, an immense Adam category B listed edifice, giving a view ahead of the Nelson Column. I walked softly between the tiny trees on either side of me afraid I might be disturbing some royal personage or other laid out in state beneath my feet but then, at the first roundabout the first thing I saw was a park cleaner. He was a smallish man wearing the usual yellow Glasgow City Council jacket and cap and was emptying the rubbish bin into a big black, plastic sack as I approached.

'Excuse me,' I said. He turned and the first thing I noticed in the morning light was the glint of his glasses. 'Can you tell me the name of those little trees that go up either side of the walkway? They're like pygmy pyramids.'

'*Taxus baccata*,' he replied without a moment's hesitation.

'What ?'

'I wis gein' ye the name of the wee topiary yews.'

'Sorry,' I went on, 'I didn't expect you to have the Latin.'

'How no?' he replied blandly.

'Of course,' I muttered lamely and was about to move away when he stopped filling the sack and peered at me through his glasses.

'Here, should Ah know ye? Yer face is kinna familiar. Whit's yer name again?'

I told him, and started to move on.

'Hey!' he called out. 'Ye've fairly pit oan the years hiv ye no?'

It was direct, but I could see the twinkle behind his thick glasses.

'Doesn't everybody?' I offered.

'Only the lucky wans.'

That stopped me. It was a point. I turned away again as he went on tying his rubbish bag. Suddenly, he said, 'Here, did ye know there's a Kearney in New Jersey?'

I was halted once more. I couldn't help smiling.

'I know, but they spell it differently.'

'Hiv ye ever been there?'

'I did a Burns show there once for the Celtic supporters club.'

'S'that right? I'm no' a Celtic man, mysel'. Imagine you bein' in America wi Rabbie, eh? By the way, did ye know, there's seven Glescas in the States?'

'No, how did you know that?'

'I read it in the li'bary. Aye, well, there ye ur. Ye learn somehin' every day, eh?'

With that he lifted his rubbish bag and carried it off to his vehicle.

I was still smiling as I watched him go. I knew I had met my match. What a lovely start to the day. Well, I'd better get on with it.

I continued up to the Nelson Column. It's not every day you meet a professorial rubbish collector. I relished the welcome he gave me nonetheless. I knew there was a rough generosity beneath the banter, and high intelligence too. He was obviously a reader. I walked on, wondering why I had never toured to one of those American Glasgows.

I came to a halt before a huge column commemorating the death of Admiral Nelson at Trafalgar in 1806. It was funded I saw by the Freemasons, theirs was that kind of Georgian patriotism. Nelson and the Duke of Wellington were the poster-boys of their age, and I'm sure Nelson, of the two, would have loved this monument had he lived. The Duke of Wellington would have accepted it as part of his duties. As he did. So I left them both to it.

I then walked over to what looked like a plain boulder set in the ground nearby. This was a very different kind of memorial. It marked the spot where James Watt had his idea about steam condensers thus giving, in effect, Britain its later Victorian railway system and Springburn its even later industry. To my mind these are greater triumphs than a significant naval victory and the death in action of Captain Horatio, a one-armed, one-eyed womaniser. I walked on, taking in the modesty of the next stone memorial on the path.

It was the 1881 fountain dedicated to Hugh MacDonald. Hugh was the first ever to write about Glasgow's parks. I stood there for a moment thinking about that then gave him a tap on his stone for being a pioneer and walked on. The entrance to the Glasshouse restaurant now lay before me, so in I went. This ample place was built within the People's Palace and Winter Gardens, a well-deserved category 'A' establishment. I found a table near the coffee counter and sat down to make some notes on events so far. I wish I had taken the rubbish man's name. Gosh, it was warm in there. I could feel the midday sun trying its best to pierce the glass dome high above my head. It was like sitting in a garden somewhere in the Mediterranean. This abundance of forest and flowers and cosy climate couldn't possibly be in Scotland, never mind Glasgow. Every kind of flower seems to be there – and from what I read, it ran from the Irish shamrock to the mystic yarrow. What lovely names.

Outside the large windows, trees that included a giant willow and a thorn tree circle that marks the spot where Bonnie Prince Charlie reviewed his Highlanders during his unlucky and badly-managed campaign for the Scottish and English Crowns – both of which, by the way, really belonged to his younger brother Henry, who was only out of the running because he was a Roman Catholic cardinal. How often clerics pop up in the Glasgow park story. Looking out and about me in this lovely situation it was difficult to imagine that it was all made possible by a small army of unemployed weavers under the command of a Mr Cleland...

Suddenly, all thoughts of Victorian dedication were dispelled by the rowdy invasion of what seemed to be half the primary school population of the East End and all in good voice and neat uniform. I couldn't help laughing at the sheer exuberance shown in the decibel level these little ones reached under that summer dome. Reluctantly, I picked up my notebook and pen and made my way through the joyful melee to the other door and continued upstairs to the Museum.

The name People's Palace encapsulates the building exactly. The Museum is the souvenir of all that's Glaswegian, especially in its pronounced political list to the left. It's a place where the voice of the people is seen if not heard and it pays compliment to the many political heroes that Glasgow boasts. There are real heroes here, men like the pacifist John Maclean from Pollokshaws, Jimmy Maxton, our East End MP and Willie Gallacher, who led the Clyde workers against the machine guns in George Square in January 1919. They showed the same courage there as the Calton Weavers had done here on this same Glasgow Green when they were martyrs to the cause of Trade Unionism so many years before. Workers today have forgotten how much they owe to the weavers in almost every town, for the rise in worker status generally was largely due to their efforts. They combined intelligence with foresight even though they themselves didn't profit much by it.

However, I was talking about a different kind of worker, the few who had survived the First World War. In the George Square incident, Black Friday, riots resulted and so serious was the situation that army tanks were called in by nightfall. Though many were hurt by batons and clenched fists, nobody died. Enough men – and women – had been lost in the needless war which had just ended, 200,000 young volunteers from Glasgow alone, more than from any other British city. This solemn undercurrent runs through every exhibit seen here in the rooms. And anger. Nonetheless, the Museum is worth a serious look for anyone interested in what makes the Glasgow character and what fires the red-lined, community passion which goes as deep as the Molendinar still lying in its metal jackets under the surrounding tailored acres.

Once out again in the open air I was immediately impressed by the sight of another Category 'A' creation, the Doulton Fountain from 1888. Built in the French Ecole des Beaux Arts style, it is in four terracotta tiers with figures on each representing the British Empire as the late Victorians saw it. The fountain was surrounded by Chinese tourists taking pictures of themselves alongside it. There is no doubt it is a formidable piece, with the statue of Queen Victoria reigning at her peak as the Empress of India. The fountain first appeared at the Great Exhibition of Industry and Science in 1888 at Kelvingrove but was relocated to Glasgow Green two years later as a personal gift from Sir Henry Doulton to the city. By 1990 it had the benefit of a 3.5 million pound regeneration scheme that restored it from weathering and vandalism, and it now stands in its prominent place in all its glory attracting tourists from all over.

I did eventually move on to admire the Children's Play Village, set up in the Greendyke St area as part of the Glasgow Green Renewal programme in 2000. Work on the park is on-going but as I walk through this particular section I can only remember the annual carnival that used to be set up every summer and the nights we East Enders spent driving dodgem cars or trying to win a coconut at the sideshows. My abiding memory of the annual carnival was the way it lit up the whole night. It drew you to it and was reluctant to let go of you to walk home in the dark via Bridgeton Cross. But a lack of city lights has never been a problem for me. For a black-out child this was normal. Stygian blackness, however, is another thing altogether. But that is rare in big cities, thank goodness. On the Green I was revelling in the late afternoon light now anticipating the gentle dusk to come.

Looking eastward, as I was doing, it was hard to miss one of the great sights of the Green – the extraordinary facade of the former Templeton's Carpet Factory. My Uncle Eddie worked there as a storeman between the wars. I never paid much attention to the place then. It was just another factory in a district of factories. The difference was that pinned across the full extent of the rear wall facing was a replica of the Doge's Palace in Venice. This impudent, but wonderful, architectural assertion in polychrome terracotta was the work of William Leiper, who was asked by the City Fathers to give the facade an artistic appearance in keeping with its position facing the People's Palace and Winter Gardens. It certainly does that. Indeed, it is almost laughable in its audacity. But you don't laugh when you first see it – you gasp. It was only when I read the story behind its 1889 construction that I fully understood its special irony. And it made poignant reading. Truth is, indeed, beyond any fiction. It appears that, in the early stages of the building, the rear wall was hit by unexpectedly strong winds and the canopy façade, then not yet fully attached to the wall of the weaving shed, was completely torn off and collapsed on top of 29 female workers, killing them instantly. The East End was aghast at the tragedy and the whole population combined to raise money for the victims' families. People poured in their pennies to the fund set up, and even the new Celtic Football and Athletic Club made a donation of £20, a reasonable enough sum in those days. On the anniversary of the tragedy in September 1954, a commemorative plaque was placed in the Templeton Memorial Garden in Tobago Street. It reads:

Green buds, for the hope of tomorrow,
Fair flowers, for the joy of today,
Sweet memory, the fragrance they leave us
As time gently flows on its way.

Once again, words do it. I walked back in a respectful silence to catch the tourist bus back to the City Centre. Those poor young women lost for the sake of mere wall ornamentation. But that's the irony of sudden accidental death; it has no sense of value.

So much for my first walk. A funereal feeling was certainly something I never expected at the end of my first park day proper. I was suddenly looking forward to that early evening glass of wine.

Tollcross Park

1897 · 83 acres

*The most common form of despair
is not being who you are*

SOREN KIERKEGAARD

THAT CERTAINLY DOESN'T apply to this author. I had no option
but to know my place, and my place in it. I had my Glasgow-ness
forged in as if by a factory furnace. My defining area of the city
was the East End, proletarian Parkhead. Despite its name, it was
all grey stone, cement and plaster, peppered by lamp posts, criss-
crossed by tramlines, cornered by pubs, overshadowed by chimneys and deafened by every kind of factory noise, yet I couldn't
have been happier there. We had no less than four cinemas in the
area, a good library not far away and, best of all, two parks within
walking distance. Westhorn, along London Road was an early
play park, but Tollcross Park, a little further away along and turning up left to its site on Tollcross Road, was the great leisure venue
for all of us, adults and children alike. It still has a strong nostalgic pull for me as it was my boyhood and early youth territory.
Perhaps the 'Park' in 'Parkhead' was the subconscious pull that
drew me to the park itself. After all, at that time it was an easy
saunter east beside the tram rails from Parkhead Cross.

Going back to Tollcross today on the No 61 bus from the City
Centre was especially enjoyable as I was joined in my double seat
by a middle-aged lady who promptly looked through her bag and
produced a sweetie bag.

Turning to me, she asked, 'Fancy a mint?'

I took one, of course, and thanked her. She popped one in her
own mouth and immediately embarked on a full explanation of
her doings that day while I sat back contentedly chewing. It was
like being back on the old tram cars again – immediate friendly
contact with whoever you landed with in the passenger seat. Pure
Glasgow, as they say.

As she chatted on, I kept my eye on the familiar city scenery
from my seat at the window, especially the giant murals painted
on the gable walls of so many tenements. This is a modern trend
and one to be applauded. Some of the pictures on stone are quite
ingenious and could even be described as striking works of art. At

any rate, they made me look twice at Glasgow buildings I thought I knew so well and realise that they really are quite striking.

Soon the bus passed the new, red-brick St Mungo's Academy in the Gallowgate and was quickly filled with exuberant uniformed teenagers of both sexes. It was touching to see the old school badge and tie again, on girls as well as boys. There were no girls at St Mungo's in my time. It was good though to see, on all these fresh, young faces, and hear too, the confidence and energy only the happy young can show. The overall sound level was only a little less than the infants managed at the People's Palace. As my mint lady said, with a grin, as she rose to leave at her stop, 'Ye cannae hear yersel think!'

My bus stop was opposite Maukinfauld Rd right at the gate to the southern end of Tollcross, where I first stood as a boy. It was here at this very gate I read for the first time: *This Park will close at Dusk*. I remember saying it aloud to myself. I just liked the sound of it, although I wasn't very sure when exactly 'dusk' was. It had a lovely, mysterious sound to it, almost a whisper, suggesting mists and half-light and shadows in which anything and everything could happen. I was given to musing about shadowed places even when very young and I've loved twilight ever since. I still think a park is the last place that should be over-lit, even by the sun. It needs hide-outs and leafy shelters to offer occasional escape because a well-planned and laid out park is pure theatre. Although, unfortunately, the enclosed spaces of Glasgow's parks have been the scenes of sadder dramas from time to time, their basic, and far larger purpose is for show and appreciation. It just occurs to me as I write this, that, still thinking theatrically, I started my professional stage career at the Park Theatre in Glasgow. I hadn't thought of that before, but of course there are theatrical possibilities in all green areas. They only need our imagination, and a show can begin.

When I was 15 years old the lights of the city had only just come on again after the war. Food rationing was still in force and austerity was the order of the day, but the park was still the park, a green alternative to our grey, urban reality, a country wonderland for a tenement boy who saw it as another world.

But what of the park now? Will it have changed and grown old

A WALK IN THE PARK

as I have? But then, parks don't grow old. They renew themselves each spring and emerge each year as they always were. A tree is always a tree, a bush a bush, and grass, thank God, will always be grass.

But I was in for a few surprises. I had just learned, for instance, that the International Rose Trial would be held in the park soon and 100 guest judges would attend to examine over 4,000 roses currently to be seen in the Rose Garden. This was certainly not the Tollcross Park I knew in the post-war years. I couldn't wait to see the re-emergent place in its new clothes. And the new roses, but then surely roses will always be roses? That's the gift of flowers. I strode out confidently with the feeling that I had just come home again. It was still my old dream place.

In my more innocent years, for instance, it was exciting to get locked in the park at night after the park keeper's closing-down whistles had blown. My pals and I had dozens of little escape holes under walls and below fences on to adjoining streets; where toffs' tidy terraced houses had their private view of the park from bedroom windows in Muiryfauld Drive to the west, from mansions in Enterkin St to the north and from the better-class tenements in Wellshot Road and Tollcross Road at the east and south. It has always been the practice of the well-to-do to build their homes in a ring round a park, another reason why so many parks were largely hidden from public view. What this also did however was to present in an East End situation some very pleasant thorough-fares beyond the main streets.

Parks were birdsong and bandstands. Though perhaps in our multi-communication age bandstands are, to most people nowa-days, not the audience-draws they once were. Uniforms and mili-tary airs may be slightly out-dated but the fact is the stands, or most of them anyway, *are* still there and they ought to be utilised in whatever acceptable manner. Although I didn't expect the notice I saw in my local park recently announcing that bicycles would receive repairs required if they were brought to the bandstand on a certain day at a certain time!

One has to remember that originally parks were created in the space available outside the industrial and commercial centre of the city. In time the city itself stretched away beyond those same park boundaries so that now these large green spaces are in the inner rim, a huge environmental advantage today. They are leisure assets to the entire city population and this is proved by how much they are used in any given year, spring, summer, autumn and winter. There is no off-season in a park, especially for dogs. Although I must say, I never saw one cat in any of the parks. Cats must think of the park as a canine reserve.

The ever-changing weather isn't always unkind and many of the parks look even better wearing their winter snow-coat. Fortunately, for the walker in Glasgow, summer snow is unheard of, (as yet!) so I had a whole, wonderfully green Tollcross Park to explore again, and I was already enjoying every minute of it. Walking up the gentle rise from the gates to the mandatory flagpole I met with my first surprise – the old shed had gone! Our old rain shelter where we would run when it poured was no more. I stood at the flagpole now and looked about me. I felt the first slight wisp of sadness.

That old shed was not only where we sheltered from the rain or hid from the parkie when he blew his warning twilight whistle to tell us that the park was closing. Its big enclosure had marvellous acoustics for some reason and that's why it was the place where we practised singing cod opera, not from the opera house but from the cinema.

I must explain – the 'we' were my three St Mungo schoolmates, Kirk, Davitt, Devlin and myself. Each of us had decent singing voices, and a real love of music, but none of us was a Mario Lanza. Yet at times we pretended we were. Because of the light tenor I had then, I landed the soprano roles. Much to my annoyance! But really, it was all just a bit of daft fun.

In a sense, the big shed was our Theatre Royal and, believe it or not, we manged a decent harmony at times, making up the words as we went along in our imitation Italian. Nobody bothered us. It was just crazy behaviour from a quartet of young teenagers huddled in the corner oblivious to everything else. As I said, it was surprisingly musical thanks to the acoustics. People hearing it as they passed by would come in now and then and remark on how nice it was to hear singing in the park even if they didn't understand a word of it. But then, neither did we. John Kirk, our 'tenor', later in life to become a big insurance executive in the United States, thought we should go round with the hat when people arrived but we never did. We preferred to be left alone to enjoy the noise we made, and keep out of sight of the parkie, as we called the man with the whistle. I gathered later that he had heard us from the start but just let us get on with our 'rheumatic songs' as he called our efforts. He had no taste for the operatic, I suppose. Didn't he know that Verdi was Italian for green, and therefore it was OK in a park?

As I stood on the hill, that was all I saw in front of me, green. Green grass on the rising ground except for what looked like a small, brown settlement in the valley below. It was the allotments. On the other side to my right over rough, unkempt grass was a black, locked building. I was told by two ladies in saris who were wheeling a push-chair that it was the sports changing rooms We didn't have changing rooms. We carried our football boots and wore our clothes on top of our team jerseys and left them in neat piles behind the goal-posts. I looked forward to seeing the old pitches again. That was the next surprise.

The ground at the top of the hill is still there but it is now completely grassed over and the football pitches have gone. I could hardly believe it. That's what Shettleston Hill was famous for – football. It was impossible for me to believe that the pitches were no longer there. They were part of our life at one time, especially for my young brother, Jim, who in fact became a professional footballer, and a good one. And it was here he first discovered that he could really play the game. In its prime, this unforgettable old sporting site must have produced many fine footballers. Now it's as if it has never been. I still couldn't believe it.

As I looked around me, I could see that also gone was my war-time St Mark's Church on the left where it faced on to Muiry-field Drive. So too the Corporation Swimming Baths where I first hated to swim. Where was half my childhood gone? Where was the old Tollcross Park? I walked on trying to shake off the disbe-lief. Then I saw a dog-walker in shirt sleeves coming towards me.

'What had happened to Shettleston Hill?' I asked him

'Hooses', he said. 'I live in wan mysel'. But the park's no' the same, know whit I mean?' I certainly did.

'Progress, I suppose,' I muttered.

Certainly, all I could see on the northern side was a very tidy housing scheme, each door with its car outside and all the appearance of comfortable living on the edge of the park. The political Wheatleys, I am sure, once lived around here. My friendly, shirt-sleeved dog-walker didn't remember them. He and I talked about the inevitable changes everywhere. The dog on the lead seemed content to listen until its owner suddenly interjected,

'Here, I know your voice, do ah no'?'

'I know' I called out as I moved away quickly, 'I've had it a while now!'

I hurried away up the hill. It was then I saw the notice by the roadside:

SILENCE PLEASE – FOR THE BENEFIT OF WILDLIFE

It was planted prominently before a copse of trees. 'That's it,' I said to myself. 'It was all a deliberate exercise'. Now I understood the reason for the unkempt grass, the scrawny bushes, the spreading trees, the loss of the pitches – not to mention the request for quiet. I had never seen that in a park before. It was all part of a deliberate attempt by the park managers to restore the natural look and atmosphere to these wide acres. There was no prim park here, no respectable municipal garden. It was a rolling green with trees and wild foliage and with a lovely natural look to it all. What brave planning, I thought, and all within reach of the running burn which acted as a kind of border between the green area where I could even see sheep grazing and the eastern side of the park where the tips of new buildings marked the other side of the park.

Now I understood why Tollcross was named as 'The Best Park in Scotland' in 2008. Astute park planning is evident here. It's called 're-wilding' – that is, reintroducing elements into available and suitable areas, extinct plants and trees and bird species so that a re-naturalisation gradually occurs. This is modern ecology at its best, and it ought to be encouraged by all who want to see the best of our world restored instead of being inevitably ruined by urban spread or climate change or whatever else is the fashionable dread.

Not that I wish to see elephants running wild on Shettleston Hill or wolves pillaging the allotments, but it would be good to be reminded by the restoration of wildlife around us that we are only scavenging animals ourselves and the instinct to do so yet is in us. We are all the basic beasts we always were, but with the advantage of added refinements as the centuries have rolled on. I had an unexpected sense of the real thing as I walked on through this 'wild side' savouring the roughness of it all and feeling elated that such forward planning can pull us back to re-consider the essentials again. Just in case we missed the point, a large notice on the main pathway told me not to get too carried away. It was the Glasgow Parks Code:

> Enjoy the trees, plants and wild life
> but please leave them for others to enjoy.
> Dogs must be kept on the lead. Please bag all fouling and bin it.
> Cyclists are welcome but please keep to pathways.

Duly warned, I kept to my pathway, nodding to people who smiled and nodded back.

A new, youthful type of park keeper passed by, not in uniform, but in smart shirt and armed with a mobile phone. He directed me to the private mansion house at the centre of the park which I well-remembered as the Children's Museum. I first learned in that old house that there were once deer in this park, about Wee Willie Winkie and his nocturnal wanderings and who it was who killed Cock Robin. It was a positive treasure trove for children in the traditional 'magic' style.

When I told the young park man why I wanted to see the Museum again, he said,

'Oh, I'm sorry, it's a care home for the elderly now.'

I could hardly believe it and, thanking him, walked towards it feeling very disappointed. How many more changes could I take? The very building itself looked sad and wistful. No doubt it is providing a valuable service but there was no magic here now. Yet, as I stood on the gravel drive, I could still hear the sound of 'Who Killed Cock Robin?' echoing from the stonework and a young child's voice answering in a way that brought back the kind of memories that are imprishable.

'I' said the sparrow, 'with my bow and arrow,

'I killed Cock Robin.'
'Who saw him die?' 'I,' said the fly.
'With my little eye, I saw him die.'
'Who caught his blood?' 'I' said the fish.
'With my little fist I caught his blood…'
And all the birds of the air fell a-sighin' and and a-sobbin'
When they heard of the death of poor Cock Robin.

It now has a second childhood ring to it. A dotage dust… Ah, well!

I made my slow way down to the familiar white bridge over the burn. At least I was glad to see that the water was still running north to south beneath, as it as it has done for centuries. I leaned on the parapet and enjoyed the few minutes of real park tranquillity. But when I glanced up I got more of a fright than a surprise. A huge white façade rose out of the left bank of the burn and its brutish modernity was thrust right into my face. I walked up to the Wellshot Road main gate trying not to look at the huge steely barn that loomed up at my side. I remembered only the flimsy wire and nets of tennis courts that once stood there. Is nothing now as it ever was? I had to admit that what I saw in front of me now was certainly of today.

It was the Tollcross Leisure Centre, a heritage from the 2014 Commonwealth games. Its uncompromising frontage was not at all inviting and, almost reluctantly I went through the circular automatic doorway – and then, yet another surprise – inside, it was really quite beautiful. I was really in another world. I had entered from all the exterior greens to find myself walking in sheer luxury over a black and white chess board floor with an airport-like roof high above and luxury fittings to right and left.

It was mind blowing, especially remembering that it was the Glasgow Club, a modern temple to physical fitness and to sport of all kinds. Within these walls, new tennis courts exist, as well as squash courts, gymnasia and any kind of muscle stimulant co-habited in what is, in effect, a scintillating resource for the healthy mind seeking the healthy body. This explained the number of cars in the car-park, and the large number of people sitting around me in the cafe. I sat sipping my coffee and munching a muffin, trying to take it all in. I noticed a huge poster on the wall showing a handless young man in a swimming costume. That, to me, summed it all up.

I sat there and considered again the two halves of Tollcross Park and how each contrast neatly underlined the other. To me, it was a perfect marriage. Two halves *can* make a whole. No doubt all the houses on the north side paid for much of it and the Commonwealth Games success here with the swimming did much to justify the extra expense in building the Leisure Centre but the overall Jekyll and Hyde effect was telling and I came out of the Centre completely revived. I had been jolted out of my old-fashioned yearning for past joys and swept into the 21st century by the Leisure Centre. It was today – so I had to seize it. I did so by ordering another coffee and gazing around me contentedly. I wished I were a schoolboy again. I wouldn't waste my time singing operatic excerpts in the big shed. I would be here trying everything the building had to offer for the care of mind and body. And I'd feel the better for it. This therapeutic element kept forcing itself on me as my promenade proceeded. I couldn't help it as my stride widened and my heart beat stronger. This was the life.

My last park target was the Rose Garden of recent fame. It was a short walk away to the right, beside the children's play park, and my first look showed me why it was an award-winner. I relished the beauty of the whole rose display and contentedly sniffed in the delightful odour. Yes, I thought, this is what parks are for, sheer sensual delight. I pulled myself away, passing the children on the swings to find my way down to the old, remembered leafy walk among the trees which led, twisting alongside the burn and towards the bridge again.

It was a calming stroll and it was here that I was made conscious of the pleasure it was, and still is, to walk under trees. Walking in the shade of trees does make you think. That's what happens in parks, thoughts come to one all the time, inspired by what is seen all round, or heard, or an emotion felt by the unexpected incident. I realised my main provoker as it were, was not the people I met, nor the beautiful aspects glimpsed. Not grass or flowers or scents, but trees. Any kind of tree, large or small, in isolation or in copses, in small forests, wherever met, and especially when they hang overhead like a protective ceiling.

As early humans, we fell out of the sheltering leaves of trees to become bipeds. We used their branches to light the first fires, and their trunks to create the first primitive shelters. In many cases, they helped provide the first sustaining fruit. In short, mankind could not have survived or developed as it has done without that miracle of growth, the tree. It has always been there, growing alongside us, saying nothing except for a creak in high winds or a crack of protest as the saw cuts them down. There were many more of them once but every year their numbers decline as the saw works continually to serve a huge commercial profit. Even the meteorological necessity of the Amazon rainforest could not save it from being mercilessly plundered, causing tribes to be scattered that have lived there from the beginning of time. At the end of my tree-walk, standing on the little bridge again, the following lines came into my head, and there and then, leaning on the parapet, I scribbled them into my notebook:

Walking under Trees

Every branch stretched out
As if it's looking for something
Letting its leaves speak for it.
As we do at times in our quest for facts
And the truth of who we are
And why?
This question has haunted humanity
Since the first 'why' splintered innocence
And left us in the dark of our mortality.
A light went out and doubt replaced old certainties.
The thesis and its antithesis
Paired to give authority a voice.
We had no choice but to yield
To news, that field of views,
Expressed by the word-makers,
Who caught their ideas in the wind
Making them suit the day
Which quickly became tomorrow
And it all began again
With matter enough to fill the void

With theories that sound good
And obviously serve the purpose.
Which is only to take our minds off the fact
That we don't know – And won't know while we live.
Meantime, we sigh
and can only wonder why
Tree trunks still rise like towers
Because of other, hidden powers
Bigger than man's puny need
And his pitiful, relentless greed.
But no money in the world can buy
The seed that grows to touch the sky.

I couldn't get rid of these thoughts. To this day, I walk under trees wherever possible letting their leaved voices speak to me as their conductor wind determines. Sometimes, it would be the creak of a small branch from just above me and I would look up instinctively not knowing what to say. Was it a greeting or a warning? Other times, there were louder noises from bigger branches and I knew then the only thing to do was quicken my pace and get back into the light and open again. Yet, I was never afraid, only cautious. I always bore in mind that many trees are bigger than us and have their own rules. It's a mistake to take them for granted. We must continue to grow them wherever possible because, as I said, they are our oldest allies and deserve our respect. As you will have gathered, I love them and enjoy their company whenever I have the chance to walk beneath them. But then, at length, at the end of a rising path, I was standing again at the flame from where this lovely trek had started hours ago – or was it years?

It had been a wonderful stretch, this revisit to old territory. It had been a whole hatful of surprises, but every one of them worth it. Three hours and 70 years had passed this afternoon, and what was I left with? An echo of blissful times in the former mansion house that was the Children's Museum in Tollcross Park, when deer roamed the grounds, and I too, was innocent and sang another kind of song as I went through the park gates again to get the bus back into town:

Wee Willie Winkie runs through the toon,
Upstairs and doonstairs in his night-goon,
Tirlin' at the windae, cryin' at the loak,
'Are aw the weans noo in their beds,
It's efter ten o'cloak!

Is it that time already? But then there is no time in dreams, and
I had been living a new dream in that ever-land I call Tollcross
Park. As it is said – Unless you become a child again...

Alexandra Park

1866 · 104 acres

No journey is too long
If it's going where we want to go,
No lesson is too hard
If it tells us what we ought to know.
No climb is too high
If it shows us what we ought to see
No hole in the ground is ever too deep
If it's there, in the end, we ought to be.

ANON 2015

WHEN MY FATHER died in 1963, I was playing in *The Rivals* at the Lyric, Hammersmith, in London and brother Jim was playing for York City in England so our mother was alone in our Parkhead room and kitchen at 20 Williamson Street. Her early widowhood was helped by her close ties with family on both sides, neighbours and close friends, but she was unsettled in what had been her married home for more than 30 years. She had always told me that she dreamed of one day living in Dennistoun, in a flat with an inside bath, so this was my chance to give her exactly that. As it happened, my next job was the lead in a BBC television serial, *This Man Craig* for which I was to be based in Glasgow for a couple of years. As soon as I was free, I flew up to Glasgow and for a whole day with my mother I walked her up and down Alexandra Parade looking for her ideal home.

We couldn't find a 'For Sale' sign anywhere, so we moved one street down, into Onslow Drive and found one opposite Whitehill School at No 197. I parked the car, and leaving my mother in her seat, I ran up the stairs to the flat concerned on the second floor to find the name 'Craig' on the letter box. This was a good omen. I thought, and rang the bell.

It was opened by a shirtless man who just looked at me steadily before grunting quietly:

'Ay?'

'I understand your house is for sale,' I said.

'Oh, ay.' He wasn't giving anything away.

'May I ask how much?' I tried to smile but it wasn't easy.

In the same laconic tone, he told me.

'Will you take a cheque?'

'Will it bounce?' the look never wavered. I shrugged.

'It's not made of rubber.' For the first time there was a grin.

'Right enough. Come in.' he opened the door and I stepped in. 'I'll get a shirt on.'

This was full extent of our negotiation and the flat was mine in ten minutes. I hurried out and bounced down the stairs two at a time to tell my mother in the car.

All she said was, 'Has it got an inside bath?'

When I told her it did her eyes gleamed and she got out of the car like a young girl. It was one of the most lovely moments of my life.

The flat had two bedrooms so that was my digs fixed in Glasgow while I was filming for the BBC. That night I caught the next plane back to London, leaving my mother with her dream come true. Her new life could begin again with a telephone, the Bingo Hall and St Anne's Church nearby, not to mention Alexandra Park, and new friends made up the same close, so she was begun on a new phase and was able to live there happily until her sudden death in 1980. May she rest in peace.

Dennistoun, with its high views of the hills all round, is on the upper rung of social standing in the East End, rivalling Hoggan-field Loch to the north. The social rungs go steadily down as you move south through Duke Street, Gallowgate, London Road and Old Dalmarnock Road and on to the banks of the Clyde. On its South Bank is the South Side, which was foreign to us East Enders. We used to call it 'Suicide' because the story is that once you went over the river you never came back. Besides, the old women said you would catch your 'death o' cauld' crossing the water at Shaw-field, so we didn't try it. Dennistoun was as far as we would like to go from Parkhead. Besides, it had something Parkhead didn't have – a park!

Except Celtic Park of course, which is now an iconic structure off the London Road at Springfield Toll, just a short walk south from Parkhead Cross or along from Bridgeton Cross walking east. It is certainly a sight worth seeing as it has developed recently, due to its position opposite the Commonwealth Cycle Stadium. Celtic Park is more than just a football ground; it is an assertion of a common ideal made by ordinary people living in this very district before the turn of the last century. It glories in green, which is appropriate here, but it is unashamedly the green of old Ireland, whose emigrants built the original ground in Springfield Road with their own hands.

Now, their descendants have lived to see this veritable sporting Vatican arise on London Road and take Celtic into the modern era. I have no shame in my pride about that because I am one of those descendants. However, that was not my concern as I made my way to Alexandra Parade once again, and, sure enough, when I got there it was exactly as I remembered it. On Parade indeed, the old familiar entrance to Alexandra Park – and what an attractive gateway it is. It is the setting for the cast-iron Cruikshank Fountain, set back from the public pavement and just before the pillared main gates, offering a Victorian welcome to the visitor. I was glad to walk in and again relive a lot of park memories, those warm shadows we all trail behind us.

The first thing I noticed were the young women, sitting on benches, talking in the sun, each with a pushchair before her or at her side. Soon both she and her charge, would be speeding through the park at a good pace either in a pack or in a long single file. This is normal park fitness practice for young maternals these days, and paternals as well, who regularly seek the open air of their parks. Good for them, and it *is* good for them. They merrily hurtled past me as I walked up the left hand side of the twin path taking me further into the interior.

I was amazed at the forest look the place had. So many of my favourite trees. It was only later I discovered there was a railway line hidden behind these same high trees. It all suggested the Berlin *Unter der Linden* with a Scottish accent. Then I saw a notice pinned to a bench. It said:

MISSING – JOHN MURPHY
From Dennistoun, Glasgow
Anyone with information
Please call Police Scotland 101

Among all this beauty and colour and peace a plain piece of paper cried out in pain from a wooden seat. Mr Murphy's picture looked out at me. A little guiltily, I turned away.

But then things like this happen in the world today. 'Poor John' I said to myself, hoping no one heard me, since I was John, myself. I was glad to move on, but I whispered a little prayer for him. As my grandmother Coyle used to say, 'Don't ever feel sorry for yourself. There's always some poor soul worse off than you.' It's good to remember that at times.

Alexandra Park has a very artistic look appropriate to the artist-filled district it serves, and this aesthetic feel is shown readily in the lay-out of the park itself. To the right the grounds stretch east all the way along Cumbernauld Rodd, hidden in summer by greenery, the distant hum of traffic just audible. Ahead of me I could just see the main art work. This was set under the hill where, formerly, audiences sat for those well-loved bandstand concerts. There's a shrub bed there now. I took the well-remembered and exquisitely manicured main pathway and found the Category 'A' Saracen Fountain designed by Watson Stevenson in 1901 and created at the Possil Saracen Works, hence its name. It was originally built for the 1901 Exhibition in Kelvingrove Park but was re-sited here in 1914 and fully restored in 2000 at a cost of £22,000. It seems worth every penny. Tom, the head gardener, whom I met on one of the intersections fully agreed. When I asked if he missed the bandstand, he said, 'No' really. Ye see, there's music here aw the time, if ye listen fur it. Know whit I mean? It's no' jist the birds, it's in the air, like.' He said this quite sincerely. He was obviously an artist too. When I said so, he shook his head, saying, 'Naw, naw, I jist get passionate. That's whit it's aw aboot, is it no'?'

I could not have agreed more and, exchanging a shake of the hand, I left him to get on with his work. I couldn't help thinking that Princess Alexandra's Park couldn't be in better hands. It was she, the future queen to Edward VII, who opened the park in 1870. The royal blessing obviously worked and this gentle, charming park-space is the result.

When my brother, Jim, and I were very young we often tried the boating pond here in the park and one day Jim fell in while we were trying to fish with empty jam jars for what we called 'baggieminnies' – small minnows. I had to 'fish' him out and walk him home, soaking wet, carrying our empty jam jars. It's a longish walk in the dusk to Parkhead via Todd Street and Duke Street to

Springfield Road but we were home before nightfall. I pulled Jim from the water but I was the one my mother scolded soundly for letting my young brother almost drown. That first memory of this park is still vivid.

Alexandra Park's official address is given as 10 Sannox Gardens, G31 3JE. It's bounded by the M8 motorway to the north, by Alexandra Parade and its continuation at Cumbernauld Road to the south, Provan Road to the east and Sannox Gardens to the west. The 'L'-shaped Sannox Gardens come off the aptly-named Viewpark Avenue and each flat has views over the park to die for. This can be seen in the sheer class of what might be, along with Kennyhill Square to its left, among the most desirable tenements in Glasgow, given that they are situated off Alexandra Parade itself. Every Eastside tenant, not only my late mother, has envied those who live here, except perhaps one old lady I met some years ago when I opened a public event celebrating the refurbishing of my old Parkhead Library not so far away near Parkhead Cross.

This elderly, bright-eyed woman told me, in an unexpected conversation I had with her, that she lived 'in a good tenement at the top of Springfield Road near Parkhead Cross' and had never been out of the East End in her life, although had visited Alexandra Park – 'Jist for the day'. She also told me she had gone to Newlands School which she could see from her room window. She worked in a local shop a few yards away in the Gallowgate until she married, which she did in a Protestant church in Burgher Street, one street away and the happy couple spent their honeymoon seeing a film 'while eatin' fish and chips at the Granada'. This was one of our four local picture-houses. Glasgow was Cinema City in the pre-war years. Churchgoing was a habit to some Glaswegians but cinema was a religion. The old lady had inherited her parents' room and kitchen and she was still living there. She never went for holidays – 'A waste o' money', but her husband took their children to Saltcoats for the Glasgow Fair Holiday with his sister and her family, leaving his wife at home. She spent her leisure hours 'At the lib'ary, in the park or at the pictures, or inaboot the hoose jist knittin' or listening to the wireless, know whit I mean? I wis happy enough.' I asked her why she had never wanted to see the world, or even more of her own city? All she said was, 'Ah wisnae that interested, honestly. Anyhow, ah hid ma ain world aw about me, if ye know whit ah mean?' I certainly did. In fact, I rather envied this extremely contented woman.

When I asked what she did for exercise she said she got all the exercise she needed by attending the housework but she did admit that she loved walking round the park whenever she could. 'I always liked walkin' through the park.' She also said, however, that her favourite park was not Tollcross Park, as might be expected, but Alexandra Park in next door Dennistoun. Occasionally, the world must have come to her all the same for she mentioned that her husband had seen the athlete, Sydney Woodison break the world mile record at Parkhead's Helenvale St Sports ground, just a few minutes away from the library. I loved meeting this lady. Her story was a genuine hermit's tale, a city hermit and there may be more of them than we might ever imagine.

That good woman, who was now a grandmother and a widow, was one of the happiest persons I have ever met. She lived her life on the inside of herself, never looking out or envying anybody, content with her given, modest lot in every way, and 'thankin' God for it'. I never knew her name, but I shall never forget her. I only hope she's still walking the good walk somewhere. But I know that, wherever she is, she'll be content.

Alexandra Park is what we might think of as a comfortable park, not too large but with 102 acres, it's not too small either. The Alex is the real thing if you're looking for the open-air experience in pleasant surroundings. It lends itself to a happy hour or so going round it at an easy pace. Like most of Glasgow's green spaces, it did not have a promising beginning. The surrounding works in the area, some of them still extant on its northern boundary, impregnated the air with oil and gas fumes and other industrial waste so that growing conditions were hardly ideal. The plants did not take kindly to the tough soil, but nature is resolute and eventually the evergreen trees and shrubs took a hold and have held their ground ever since. Problems of industrial pollution were once common to many Glasgow parks but they have long been solved.

Today, in the geo-spaces all parks are, we see holly and rhododendron bushes excelling in the contemporary earth along with the deciduous trees and almost everything else in the planting

A WALK IN THE PARK

structure. There are no more pools of sludge, or 'shitey oceans' as they were called by the ordinary folk who had to live with them on occasions. The park's contemporary class was only made possible because of the battle won by the plants over the chemical legacy created by the huge St Rollox factory nearby built by Charles Tennant and family, which made gardening of any kind a hard job at best. It was only by sheer determination and the generosity of Mr Tennant that ground was made available at Sighthill and gradually the sludge and the waste were removed and the inhospitable soil was completely rejuvenated. Trees, bushes and flowers were grown, from which everyone can benefit now.

Generally speaking, parks are worth the trouble they cause to create, not only because they provide an amenity and for increasing the attractiveness of the area but also because they offer a welcome alternative to soot and smoke, and that is vital to health and well-being. Alexandra's highest points give splendid views of Ben Lomond and the Tinto Hills and there is also the bonus of plant life, which in all its variety and colour, shows the quality it shares with the Glasgow people themselves, a companion resilience to dirt and squalor. You can't help being smudged from time to time, but that doesn't mean you're dirty.

One point to bear in mind in this regard is that, once again, it was the poorer citizens themselves who laboured to build this richly-endowed resource. During the great Trade Depression in the 1860s, hundreds of unemployed artisans, hungry and penniless, were glad to earn an honest shilling by lending a hand to the City Council in order to make another park. Walter Stewart of Haghill, the original owner of the land would hardly recognise the place – which he would have known as Wester-Kennyhill – particularly as Mr Alexander Dennistoun, proprietor of the adjoining five-acre estate of Golfhill at the west corner of the park, likewise made a gift of it to Glasgow. This was the generous gesture that gave the surrounding district its name. Naturally, Golfhill became a golf course.

Other gaming pursuits available here include four bowling greens, two children's playgrounds, a games court, an orienteering course, a picnic area and the inevitable outdoor fitness gym which was installed in 2013. I must say, the Alexandra pond is not as filled with home-made boats (and jam jars) as it used to be. However, as you will see, the park still has the dignity and style, qualities which so fit the environment it shares with Dennistoun itself. As I saw when I took a southerly descent from the top of the that led me back to the main gates on the Alexandra Parade.

Looking along the old Parade again I could see why Dennistoun is now finding its place as Glasgow's new artists' quarter. It lends itself naturally to the artistic, which is why there are so many studios and work-places in the surrounding streets. James Salmon (Senior) was the original architect for most of this desirable East End development in the mid-19th century and it shows his stamp. The atmosphere in its many little squares is subtly Parisian, not only due to the influx of artists in recent years but to the residual feel of the architecture seen on every corner. The modern Market Gallery at its centre is run by the artists themselves and should be visited. It's an art hub along the Parade at the point where it used to be called 'Tobacco Road' because of the Wills cigarette factory which once dominated the area. It made the Woodbine cigarette which sustained so many young men through two World Wars.

The factory is now an art amenity itself. This is no more than just, as Glasgow's most famous artist and architect, and designer of its iconic Art School, Charles Rennie Mackintosh was brought up at 2 Firpark Street, a tenement building in Dennistoun, and his first school was Mr Reid's Public school there, before moving on to Alan Glen's Academy, as it was called then, in the city in 1875. A more modern artist/author, of some status too, is Alasdair Gray, also a Dennistoun man and noted for his epic novel, *Lanark* as well as for his many murals around the city. *Lanark* was ten years in the writing, by the way, before being published in 1981. There's aesthetic thoroughness for you.

Yes, Dennistoun might be the very place to live if you want to do so with a paintbrush in hand or a pen at the ready. You will join a welcoming tribe. If you do, make sure that you invite all of them to join you in a walk round Alexandra Park on the first fine day.

Hogganfield Park

1920 · 123 acres

Golf is a good walk spoiled.

MARK TWAIN

WHEN I WAS A young teenager I might have agreed with Mr Twain because, on good days, my brother and I walked all the way to Hogganfield Loch Park from Parkhead with our Father to play golf at Lethamhill – or rather for me to watch the two of them play. I preferred to sail on the hired boats on the Loch, where I was a little more at home. Anyway, we would march all the way up Cumbernauld Road towards Millerston, Jim and I sharing the carrying of the Golf Bag which only contained the necessaries – a driver, a putter and two irons, a three and a nine, which we also shared. Lethamhill is on the right and is laid out along the south-ern shore of Hogganfield Loch in Hogganfield Park to which it is linked as an amenity.

Like other Glasgow parks, Pollock Country Park for instance, Hogganfield is a twin, almost a triplet, consisting as it does of a golf course, a massive boating pond and adjoining on its north side, a more than ample nature reserve. Quite an area to cover in a day, I thought, but I would see what I could take in. Of course, I knew the Loch well. As a youth, I was attracted to the boating, but as I grew older I took up golf, or rather the golf bag, because, as I said, it was my brother and my father who really played the ancient Scottish game. My father was a member at Lethamhill and it was there that I began my acquaintance with the 'gowf' as he called it jokingly.

Lethamhill is still a very popular course, much frequented as it is by locals, as it was by brother Jim, because he really was a good golfer even as a boy. I wasn't even an efficient caddie but I would sometimes play when allowed. Dad was an excellent golf tutor, as he proved with Jim; I was his one failure. I must confess that all my life I have studied hard to be helpless at things I didn't enjoy. The only benefit from my not playing, was that we saved a lot of time, and I was just glad to take in the scenery. Which is an aspect of golf often overlooked. It is a superb introduction to nature and its always-available attractions.

However, despite Mark Twain, I did enjoy the walk – and the

talk. Dad could be quite funny at times. In a few years, Jim, because of his early success as a footballer, was able to buy himself a full set of golf clubs, and later he bought our father the same. He didn't offer to do likewise for me. I didn't mind. I inherited the original skeleton set, and I've no idea what happened to it, though I know what happened to Dad's. The bag spent a lot of weekdays in the Glasgow Cross pawnshop during rough times on the work front. I didn't mind missing out on golf. Although I admit it is excellent taken in fresh air and among beautiful scenery and in the fresh air.

And what better air is there than in a park, and where else would one expect such good scenery? Especially when the park, like Hogganfield, has the extra bonus of wide, adjacent water. It almost makes it a seaside course in the old, traditional links manner. Oddly enough, nowadays I really enjoy watching golf being played on television. I find it absolutely relaxing and absorbing. Perhaps this is only a throwback to early days as a golf spectator at Lethamhill?

Ironically, in a long acting career I was only twice required to play golf. Once for television in New Zealand as a priest who was mad on the sport and once, even earlier, on Ealing Golf Course in a commercial for Prize Crop cigarettes. As a Scot, I managed to convince the English director that I really knew the game we had invented. I even holed a very long put at one stage, only because I had actor's luck during the action. After all, I was playing a good golfer in front of the camera, even if it were only for a commercial. But the right mental attitude works every time. I was hired as a great golfer so 'great' I had to be. I remember the director asked me where I had learned the game? I was tempted to say, 'St Andrew's' but instead, I replied without a moment's hesitation: 'Lethamhill'.

I don't think I've handled a golf club since.

It was nearly lunchtime when I arrived at the gates of Hoggan-field Loch Park. No giant stonework here, nor any impressive archway, merely a wide opening off the roadway that let the cars, the golfers and the walkers like me, enter freely. I stood with a group of people who took in the wonderful scene that opened up before us on the loch. Behind a wire fence, a gaggle of geese squabbled among themselves while some enormous swans looked on, all anxious to get to us, or rather to whatever we might have brought for them to eat. Tidbits were indeed thrown from all around me as we stood at the water's edge. The crowd shouts only added to the racket created by the scrambling of these big birds.

I hadn't heard such a din since Saturday nights at the old Metropole. I stood amazed when, all of sudden, as if on a signal, the swans ceased to clamour and in a swift about turn, they speedily made off across the immense pool of water behind them, the ducks trailing dutifully after. They had been fed so the crowd dispersed around me. I was left on my own, holding a piece of bread I picked up. So much for my reintroduction to Hogganfield Loch.

Hogganfield was formerly known as Frankfield Loch, which supplied water to local mills. In 1920 it was bought by Glasgow Corporation and developed in conjunction with the adjacent golf course and eventually created the impressive space that is the present park. By 1926, the water level was deepened and, by the artificial application of soil, a new island emerged at its centre. The surrounding waters were given over to the hired boating which I can remember well. Jim and I, with an oar each, made a habit of going round and round in never-ending circles but at least, that time, he managed not to fall in. Motor boats were also available but we could never afford that luxury. East Enders are not natural sailors but I have no memory of any accidents or drownings. The boating was later withdrawn and the island became, in time, a designated Bird Sanctuary and habitat, now one of Hogganfield's main attractions. This eventually led to the park's being declared a Local Nature Reserve in 1998. Consequently, the island has been left undisturbed in order to encourage wild life of all kinds, but particularly birds, of which there are no shortage, as I found out for myself further on in my walk. I had anticipated an uninterrupted circuit of the loch but when I saw a man lying prone on the embankment, I had to halt.

Thinking he was injured, I tentatively moved nearer. Then I saw he was actually filming two tower-tall Whooper Swans who were standing like sentinels pointing their lengthy yellow bills at the footpath. I saw why as I drew nearer. Between the Mother and Father Whooper was the neatest square of offspring, furry and velvety, snuggled into each other on the grass, their little heads whirling around in curiosity. I counted eight – Whooper octuplets, no less – each identical to the next, and making altogether the most charming of pictures. No wonder the cameraman was busy.

The Whooper parents didn't seem to mind him, nor did they worry about their chicks. I stepped backed. I had no wish to spoil the picture. I sat down at the next bench and watched. There was also, as I sat on that bench, the concomitant pleasure suggested in the readily available sight of passing humanity. This was the great park mobile cabaret which unfolded on the broad pathway before my eyes and very much in my ears.

First came a determined, well-dressed elderly lady with eyes only for what lay ahead of her. Not a glance did she give right or left as she slowly ran with all the dignity a life of correctness had given her. She was followed by an equally senior couple, twin-hatted, wearing thick plimsolls, stepping it out smartly in unison, and never a word between them. They were followed by another lady, this time in a cardigan, who gave me a smile as she passed. I smiled in reply but she was already past me. It was only then I noticed that I was sitting at the authorised angling zone so I got up quickly before I was hooked myself and carried on walking.

Two smart young women soon passed me talking together as women do, both moving their lips simultaneously yet each appearing to hear every word of what the other said. This is a very feminine skill but I couldn't help thinking, why should they bother to come out in such a lovely setting and not even give it a glance? Well, that's their way, and they seemed to be thoroughly enjoying it. Two men were next, one small, one tall, with the small one doing all the talking. The tall one just nodded from time to time. And so the carnival of walkers went on. I did notice a line of houses and a water-tower on the horizon ahead to remind me that I was still in Glasgow. In a striking location like this you can soon forget a huge city lies just over the nearest fence. This is especially so when one is part of the pedestrian parade of nods, smiles and hand-waves.

Continuing my own walk, I came to the top of the loch and took the opportunity to sit again and look around. It was extremely satisfying. Water always is. Looking over this wide expanse, I thought that life was couldn't be better appreciated than it is beside water of any kind. It is impossible not to feel peaceful when watching

A WALK IN THE PARK

water flow, whether it's a gurgling stream, a mighty river or even high waterfall. Moving water can't fail to suggest energy and that's always reassuring. It is irresistible. Why is this so? We all know that water in full power and expanse can be dangerous, even fatal. It can bring down towers and waste great stretches of land, drowning everything it meets in the process, yet there is nothing we like better than to sit comfortably in the sun and gaze on water, the more expansive the better. What is so therapeutic about hydrogen oxide?

Perhaps it's because it's so vital to life itself in so many ways and so natural to us that we take it for granted, except when it is in short supply of course, like in a desert or on top of a mountain. Fortunately, Hogganfield is neither. This particular stretch encloses its own island and at my feet was a beach of real sand that, to me, suggested New Zealand's benign coast line. The water looked swimmable. This thought was immediately contradicted by the notice saying, 'NO SWIMMING'. I didn't really mind; I don't swim well.

Two men passed me next, one small one tall and the small one was doing all the talking. It was then I suddenly realised I had seen them once already, going the opposite way, this meant that they had made a full circuit of the loch while I had sat here. I rose quickly, feeling slightly shamed and resumed my own steady stroll. I had dallied too long at the loch edge. To move at the pace of the wee man and keep up a running commentary at the same time would signify a reasonable fitness, or at least a determination to get something off his chest. I carried on in my own trail and came across a printed notice telling me that this site was known during the 2014 Commonwealth Games in Glasgow as a hub park. This was only right because the whole place would easily lend itself to any open-air activity because there is a whole sea of possibilities around the loch. There is every form of life in and around it. I could see it for myself as I gazed about on my walk.

From the well-heeled golfers at the fringe, the walkers of every size and style on the pathway and meanwhile, in the air, birds flying in from every possible country. However, there was one species I never saw, that bird particular to Glasgow – the wee cock sparra. Nor did I hear a cuckoo. Otherwise the whole area seemed a positive and comprehensive birdland. Every kind of migrant bird was there, not to mention every kind of insect – apart from the midge, or 'midgie' as we called it. In the water were ducks of great variety with giant swans and fish sharing it with them. Everything lives in this park from wildfowl to skylark to water vole. I wondered how they all got on together. Probably just like us. Good and bad – you keep out of my nest and I'll keep out of yours. But I could see no sign of a vulture or a raven. Thank God! I made the homeward turn without attempting to lose myself in the wild.

There were alternative narrow paths one might take that lead to green pleasures, but I stuck to the wider tarmac one I knew would lead me back to the main road. Meantime, I could enjoy the stroll. In a sense I supped from every flower, bush and tree on the way. There was woodland, marsh and grassland all around me – ample space for every taste. Life pulsated wherever I looked and only my diminishing leg energy stopped me going even further through these heavily populated acres. I was highly relieved when I finally came to the main exit again.

I stood at the bus stop at the entrance and waited – and waited. At length, I grew impatient and, since it was a lovely night, I decided to walk on down to the next stop. Of course as soon as I moved away from the bus stop my bus came roaring past me. I felt its slipstream and edged to the side but I kept walking – and walking – and walking... until, as John Clare said, I 'walked out of my knowledge' of Hogganfield Loch Park.

As night-time fell darkly all around me I was still walking, and found, to my great surprise that, in the fading hours of the day, I had walked all the way through the East End and over the Clyde into the Gorbals. I caught a bus from outside the Citizens' Theatre and in no time I was standing at my own front door. I think I must have had a fit of walking hysteria. I just couldn't stop. I didn't mind. I had caught a bit of park fever and I knew I would soon sleep it off contentedly. I couldn't wait for bath and bed but as I settled down to sleep – I don't know why – I couldn't get poor John Murphy of Dennistoun out of my mind.

Had he walked – and walked – and was he still walking somewhere?

A WALK IN THE PARK

Springburn Park

1892 · 77 acres

True wisdom is in knowing what you don't know.

CONFUCIUS

I KNEW I WAS going into foreign territory when I saw the name of my destination on the train from Queen St that morning. *Alit an Fluairaina* it said in print above my head and I presumed this was Gaelic (or *Gaidhlig*) for Springburn, a working and middle class district to the north of *Ghlaschu* or Glasgow. Certainly the name has a strong other-race feel, still very Scottish but not the accepted traditional Irish root, which is the other immigrant contribution to Glasgow's working-class character. Sitting there, reading signs in an unknown tongue it made me think of the current situation for refugees all over Europe and the sad flight of so many innocents from the religious wars in the Middle East.

It almost seems that a sick Middle East is vomiting at every port on the Mediterranean and no one is cleaning up the mess. The inhuman pile-up at borders has caused more deaths than many of the great battles in history, and the disgrace of it all is compounded by the manner in which other so-called civilised nations are dealing with the on-going situation. There may be political and criminal reasons for its happening but most of these people justly want to get out of the way of the bullets. For many, centuries of previously solid infrastructure, tribal loyalties and family lines have been totally destroyed.

No doubt sheer pity and common sense will win through in the end, but in the meantime, it is a very sad and painful situation for so many, God help them.

To a very much lesser extent of course, but this same problem of sudden immigration affected Glasgow in the late 18th and early 19th centuries, when the blunt takeover of the Highlands by non-Scottish landlords forced so many local families to emigrate to Canada, America, Australia, New Zealand and to Glasgow, which was then the Second City of the Empire. Naturally, the Highlanders settled in the first place they came to in the city, which was on the north side in what we now call Springburn.

In the older Glasgow this was the land of wild Highlandmen who spoke a foreign language and kept themselves to themselves.

'Springbuggers' was how we East Enders referred to them – in a friendly way, of course. We didn't know them after all. We didn't understand that these strong, reserved people were not only Glasgow Northerners but Scottish Northerners, people who boasted a proud independent streak firmly held within a clan-based tradition. Not to mention a deep religious centre, which was also a part of their tartan make-up. This strong Highland seam in their ancestry is still in 'Springbuggers' today, and they are proud of it.

Many of the clans lost their traditional homes not to wars, religious or otherwise, but to the moneyed land-grabbers in post-Jacobite times. For ordinary people thereafter, the mountains were theirs no more and there was no longer space down in the glen. As a result, they came south in their tartan hordes and restarted in the growing Glasgow. They kept to the heights, as it were, holding the high north of the city as their own from the beginning. Perhaps they felt that by looking over their shoulders from time to time they could see, if only through the mist of memory, the old places they had been forced to leave. Most Glaswegians know well this sense of bond between people and place, and the new, northern Glaswegians were no different about their heather heritage. Despite being abruptly exiled, they were to provide for the growing city a calibre of worker and technical tradesman that was to change the face of the district and Glasgow at large in the years to come. Springburn came to be recognised, between the wars, as the engine-room of Glasgow and it was, without doubt, the industrial workshop of the world.

The area is still heated by these same furnace flames, as it were, and affected by ever-turning wheels. Nevertheless, what we have to remember first is that it has something of real historical and geological interest in its solitary park on which also hangs on a religious event of major importance to Scotland, never mind Glasgow. The historical fact is that Kentigern's pre-Glasgow was begun in this area, on this very earth and stone, so it is plain that the place had a holy, satisfactory start. It was all this that gave me the feeling of going north, venturing into strange territory. On arrival at the Springburn Railway station exit I was soon pointed on my way to the park by a passer-by in his terse, Springburn way – 'Take a right up Balgray-hill Road tae the tap. Ye cannae miss it.' And he went on his way.

I started up the hill as directed, summoned by a couple of pink skyscrapers I could see dominating the horizon to the right. They were like two great fingers beckoning me upwards. On my left, buried in a bowl of trees, is the Springburn Centre, yet another commercial village given a sylvan setting in which to attract the customer's car and his or her credit card. I am not at all tempted but take advantage of the bus stop at the top to have a seat and catch my breath and take in the wonderful view. I had the extraordinary feeling that I was walking on the roof of Glasgow. There is greenery everywhere in Springburn, even on the gable walls of tenements. This is as effective as any mural in my opinion. The high windows on either side must have a telescopic view of the city beneath them and the highest points must surely have some of the best all-round views in Glasgow, I had to remind myself that among the charming villas ahead; on the same road bordering the park lies the very first house designed by Charles Rennie Mackintosh, no less. At 140 and 142 Balgrayhill, they represent Toshie's first attempt at an architectural project while in his first year with Honeyman and Keppie and still attending night classes at the old Art School. In 1890, he was asked by his Uncle Willie (William Templeton) to design a house. He was given two houses, but even here in what was otherwise a modest semi-detached mansion, the Mackintosh flair was shown by his placing the main doors of each, not at the centre of the facades facing the road but at the sides of the building thus making it easier for carts and carriages, and later, the car and the goods van to enter on the driveway. As a Mackintosh devotee, I really ought to take the time to look at them. I made a note to do so after I had attended to my first priority – Springburn Park.

There are no great pillars here, or pointless ornamentation, merely a plain, workmanlike gate indicating the entrance. I went through and before me was another gate, again plain, but carrying, in large, white letters, the simple announcement: 'Springburn Rockery'. It was almost deliberately unostentatious, like the rest of Springburn, yet somehow it felt right. Here I was, fresh from a train that took me from the city centre, standing on the very soil that greeted the founders of Glasgow all those centuries ago and that was a good enough feeling for me. It was a lovely moment of realisation and I drew it in with a deep breath. Thus encouraged, I made my way up to the Rockery, walking over its little iron bridge and found myself crossing into another world.

What I had learned on my park walks so far was that every park is its own experience and no two are ever the same, but I wasn't prepared for this corner of Springburn. This wasn't a park; it was another country. It wasn't green, it was pure, brown rock face. A miniature Grand Canyon. It was astonishing. On one side it was Monet's *Water Lillies*, dark green and voluptuous, and on the other, light green grass emerging from yellow water as if from a more modern school. I leaned on the bridge trying to take both sides in. It was the rocks straight ahead that eventually drew me away to explore further.

The rock garden may have been an old quarry in 1892 but thanks to the then Glasgow Corporation it has become a sculpted sight to behold. It was only recently refurbished yet again with the assistance of the Friends of Springburn Park. Good luck to them. This place I was standing in is more than a primitive beauty spot. It is a voice calling from Glasgow's beginnings. It resonates with the rumble of centuries, the tolling of bells, the sound of monks in prayer. For all our sakes, these prayers were answered in the foundation of a simple monastery which gave way in time to a centre of pilgrimage, a huge medieval cathedral and the gradual emergence of a great city which built it.

When the Romans arrived in what they called Caledonia in AD 83 they were unable to settle in what is now Strathclyde, not because of any Pictish resistance but because of an even more defiant enemy – the midgie. The little pest infiltrated into parts of the legionnaires' armour which no one else could reach and eventually caused these seasoned warriors to retreat from this putative part of the Holy Roman Empire. It was left to another holy individual, the young Celtic monk called Kentigern to pick up where the military had left off and begin a cycle of events that led to the eventual founding of Glasgow. It is not known whether or not he was impervious to midgies!

What is known is that he had only stopped in the area to find water for the two oxen which were dragging the cart which was carrying a dead body. This was Fergus, his superior in the Cowie monastery near Kincardine in Fife from which they'd travelled days before. Fergus had asked to be buried wherever the oxen stopped on the journey west and on this very hillside was the place they did. Kentigern travelled across Scotland from Fife and, led by the oxen to this spot, duly interred his fellow-monk and watered the animals. Then, no doubt on a fated impulse, he decided to stay.

Kentigern, or Mungo as he came to be known, was by birth a royal foundling, a Prince of Strathclyde incidentally, whose mother was Queen Enoch. She had been rescued from the wrath of the King by St Serf and with her child was given shelter in the monastery in Culross in Fife where Kentigern received his education and later became a monk himself. This is when he was given the name Mungo, meaning 'dear one'. It was he who built a small chapel around the grave of his superior and when he was later joined by monks from Fife they built a larger chapel down the mountainside nearer the river and beside the tiny hamlet of houses called Glasgow that was there already.

Eventually, as history records, the chapel became a church and, as Mungo's fame grew, a place of pilgrimage. All that the monks had done was follow the course of the stream which had originally given water to the oxen. This was the Molendinar Burn which went all the way down the mountain until it joined the Clyde in the south. Later people then began to widen the waterway so that mills were powered and the first industry in Glasgow was established. It was St Ninian, the first Scottish saint, who was much later to build the famous Glasgow Cathedral which still stands proudly off the High Street in modern Glasgow under the shadow of the Necropolis.

And all this happened because of a royal warrior-monk with two names, who in serving his God unwittingly founded a city and gave it its motto – 'Let Glasgow Flourish'. We can now understand the relevance of this motto's former continuation – 'by the preaching of His Word and the praising of His Name', but there is a school of thought that it also translates this as 'the Family' which is just as valid when one consider the familial character of its monastery beginnings. It could also be a Welsh inclusion since Mungo spoke Welsh as well as Gaelic as his later time with his protégé, St Asaph, in Llanelwy, Wales, showed. Mungo was a pilgrim there as much as he was in Glasgow and Celtic links are still strong between the two countries, if only in language.

Glasgow is still a place of pilgrimage but the present day pilgrim is the football fan or the modern music disciple or the ordinary tourist drawn to the city from all over the world. And it all sprang from a trickle of water issuing from a rock face in what is now Springburn. Why doesn't the pilgrim today come here to the Rockery? What was it, I wondered, that the first holy men saw as they looked down from where I was standing? No doubt it was of a heavily wooded mountain-side studded with rocks and leading down to the river and beyond that to the sea away to the right. And from nearby Cardowan, the Molendinar Burn, which started it all, still trickles down to the Clyde.

It was hard to take that it was in these surrounds, that centuries later, the kilt was exchanged for the dungarees and a whole new life was begun in Springburn for so many. The trees surrounding me now seemed bigger from where I sat than the protruding skyscrapers. I rose and walked up and round to the top of the rock face and looked down and around me. I could see no one anywhere. I didn't mind. I had no need of company here. This location had its own ghosts and they were all benign. I knew I wasn't really all alone, standing as I was on top of a city. Even the traffic noise from the hidden roadways was diminished to a hiss by the abundant foliage all round me. I took a deep breath and then sucked in the silence, letting it wash me clean. I felt genuinely privileged to be there at that moment – and alone.

The atmosphere reeked of ancient days. I couldn't shake off the strong sense of history in the place. Here I was sitting in what was merely the reworking of a disused stone quarry yet it spoke to me strongly of another people at another time. The only way now was to go was deeper into their space, into this park. So I turned away and headed for the usual tarmac path I could see below me and let it lead me where it would.

I was now walking along what can only be called 'Les Champs de Springburn', such was its elegance. It was almost Parisian, a wide thoroughfare, named the Birch Avenue naturally, because of the birch trees lining it as it leads to the Reid Statue. Sir James

A WALK IN THE PARK

Reid was one of the early industrialists who had brought the Hyde Park Locomotive Works to the area in late Victorian times and was also a contributor to the creation of Springburn Park. He lived in nearby Belmont House and his sons were later to assist with the 1900 extension of the park. An even earlier resident in the park's present space, as mentioned earlier, was William Moses, an 18th century merchant who made his fortune selling sedan chairs. The commercial instinct was always strong in the north. His house later became a manse. What is less known is that it was in that this manse that the motor car made its Scottish debut in Springburn. This was thanks to the ingenuity of the minister's son, George Johnstone. It was he, with the backing of Sir William Arrol, who produced the Arrol-Johnstone car in 1895 from Mosesfield yard and continued to do so for the next 30 years. The firm was called 'Mo-Car' but funds soon ran out and Glasgow lost its chance to create a Mac car for the world. What a coup that would have been. The manse-built Mo-Car. A big chance missed. The house is now an old men's club.

I continued my walk further into the welcoming, widening, open green space and found myself the unwitting eavesdropper to a park conversation. Two women, one middle-aged, one younger, were talking as they came towards me. The elder was appearing to comfort the younger, who was looking a little red-faced. I couldn't help hearing what the elder woman was saying as they came towards me.

'Ye never know, hen. Ye mighta done somebody a bit o' good they dinae expect.' The younger replied, almost tearfully,

'Ah've never loast my purse afore. It musta drapped oot ma bag.'

And, as they were passing me, she pulled the younger one nearer to her.

'Well, it's no' as if ye loast an airm or a leg, is it?'

They passed under the birch trees without giving me a single glance. I thought, how wonderful they should be so engrossed. They didn't look like mother and daughter, more like aunt and niece, but what was refreshing was that such a sensible philosophy should be overheard in a park – that nothing is a real calamity if you have survived it, and that one person's bad luck can be another's good fortune. All in a few lines as if discussing the weather. Great.

I was still pondering this bit of folk wisdom when I came across a cairn giving full details of the route taken by the Nature Trail. It seemed extensive enough to judge by what I read of its ponds, woodlands and meadows and other conservation intentions. I didn't think that was in my remit today however. No, I thought, life's too short, I already had that very pleasurable natural moment at the Rockery. That was enough for me. I walked on.

Then, to my delight, the Peace Garden revealed itself set out neatly on a level plain with its Peace Pole prominent. It was donated to Glasgow by Japanese survivors of the first atomic bomb. What a stark remembrance in this gentle, still atmosphere. A silence only broken by the sound of children laughing in the playground just across the meadow-like expanse lying before me. And what a contrast, a reminder of all the sophisticated, industrial enterprise put to the process of wiping out a Japanese city and most of its people. Yes, it was a strategy that worked and no doubt precipitated the end of the Second World War, but at what a cost?

Now a simple pole memorial reminds us of all those deaths, and what war costs in lives for just another military victory that is already merely a historical statistic. The irony is that this space now given by the Japanese survivors is in the centre of a district famous then for its engineering skills, which were just as sophisticated in their time as the atom bomb in 1945. It makes little difference that the people sacrificed were people just like those I could now see all round me – one lady walking, one runner running, one old man sitting and a horde of young children zipping about and shouting in the play park with parents, teachers and minders. The noise they made – the children I mean – is the best park music one can hear.

I let it sing in my ear as an anthem to my uneasy World War Two thoughts and turned to the right intending to return to the exit gates. Instead, another Springburn ruin reared up before me – its huge Winter Garden in the Park. It stopped me dead. It is a magnificent construction even though it only exists today in rusting, skeletal form. This is a Grade 'A' listed building just as Mosesfield House is, but it is not in the same good shape. The Winter Garden edifice has been derelict for more than 20 years and it is hoped that funds may yet be found to restore it one day.

It so deserves to be brought back to life, if only as a monument to the Springburn men and women who have given the district its special name as a base for high industrial efficiency and workmanship.

One has only to think of the Arrol motor and the ubiquitous locomotive railway engine which went everywhere in the world out of factories within a mile of this same Winter Garden. Why not, in the new scheme of things already being considered for the district, resurrect the Gardens as the Springburn Museum of Engineering and draw on specimens worldwide? After all, didn't James Watt have the original idea for the steam engine on Glasgow Green and George Johnstone his motor car idea in his home in these very park grounds? Surely the Friends of the Park could rally round this happy circumstance?

They would find that they had many more Friends than they thought around the world, where the figure of the Scottish engineer is venerated yet.

The district that bred him was the one that was at the root of the city that gave his ancestors a home but it also gave space to the Springburn native in his factory working on anything which moved by turning a wheel or pulling a lever and not just pressing a button. Glasgow should honour this line by creating something in this park by which we can remember this admirable and unique artisan. Cowlairs was not only the local football team once upon a time, it was the name of the workshop here, a badge of superiority earned by a new stream of workmen who were establishing Springburn as a complete industrial identity, producing results that were enjoyed worldwide, particularly with the spread of railway lines in every country of the British Empire. These weren't quite Golden days for the proletariat but they were shining silver as each locomotive train rolled off the assembly line. The age of travel was just beginning and the people of Springburn were among the first to get it going.

Nowadays the world, unfortunately, is getting nearer and nearer to a sedentary, robotic co-existence with the super-sophisticated social media with all its communication cousins, at the pinnacle of modern engineering. The level of technical efficiency worldwide has never been higher with everyone having hand-held outreach to everyone else on the planet. Whether this is a good thing or not sociologically is not the point here, but one really has to wonder where the personal touch has gone? Facebook is not exactly living face to face is it? Today's green park, and the personal exchange it offers, could be perhaps a timely brake to this trend. However, these thoughts were mere digressions as I completed my park walk.

I was now completely obsessed by how the Springburn Park Winter Gardens area might be brought back to life. What a feat of modern engineering it would be to restore it as a viable working entity. It could really make 'Made in Springburn' mean something again. Meantime, the park has its particular memories. How I would have loved to have thumbed a lift on the way out from young Mr Johnstone's Mo-Car in order to catch a Springburn-built locomotive back into Queen Street. Instead, I walked all the way back down Balgrayhill Road to the station. I realised it was now almost too dark to turn around and search out the Mackintosh semi-detached at Numbers 140 and 142. So, apologising to Toshie, I kept moving downhill. Everything is downhill from Springburn Park.

Botanic Gardens

1891 · 42 acres

The smallest point can win the biggest game.

ANON

MY PARK TARGET today is the smallest on my list. It is known locally as the Botanics, but its formal title is the Botanic Gardens. I wonder if it ought to be Botanical? Whatever it is, the Gardens can proudly claim to have, despite its size, an incredible variety of interest and attraction behind its gates. It is also the most central city park as it is situated right at the junction of Byres Road with Great Western Road in the West End and everyone knows how valuable that situation is as far as public access and awareness are concerned. In other words, the Botanics are posh!

The Botanic Gardens represents a privileged view to the south of the West-End, highly trendy Byres Road commanded at the top corner by the Oran Mor, a former Kelvinside church but now a restaurant and theatre complex famous for its Play, a Pie and Pint every lunch time and packed houses at night for up-date performances of every kind of show-piece. Byres Road itself, or the Byres, so called because it once held the sheep that once grazed on Broomhill, is the nearest thing Glasgow has to Montmarte where student-land vies with privilege to make the area a place to be if you are arts-minded and can afford be choosy. The Ubiquitous Chip speaks for itself as the vanguard of eating-places available at hand although the Western Infirmary is no longer available at the foot of Byres Road in case of emergencies! It is now part of the Glasgow University campus.

Great Western Road, at the top of the Byres, runs east to west alongside the park and is the last haven of the good house in the good street to be found so near the City Centre. It hides itself shyly behind trees but Great Westerners know who they are and where they are even if the curtains are kept drawn. Meantime, the Gardens nestle behind a line of charming cottage-type buildings shielding the main gates and they hold up their Victorian pince-nez to look across the traffic lights and to the busy world beyond. This is a park that knows its own worth; it boasts a fine pedigree starting from its beginnings in 1817 when the original eight-acre Botanic Garden was founded by Thomas Hopkirk of Dalbeth at nearby Sandyford.

Glasgow University greatly assisted in its botanical progress, as its Regius Professor of Botany, WJ Hooker was particularly active in this respect for the next 20 years. He then left to become Director of the Royal Botanical Gardens at Kew, in London but he kept an eye on his old responsibility and willingly offered advice and assistance whenever required. In this way, the Gardens progressed and developed to such an extent that in 1842 they were forced to move to a larger site which was the present Kelvinside.

At first the Gardens were open only to members of the Botanical Society but eventually the public were allowed in at the cost of one penny. I checked my loose change while I stood in the queue at the traffic lights waiting to cross to the main gates. I had a good view of the number of people going through the gates. The percentage that seemed to be non-Glaswegians was telling. It was a fine sunny morning but even so the crowd of people gathered at the entrance was impressive. I only hoped there was room for one more. Seriously though, I was really looking forward to this trek. Although I had visited the Kibble Palace many times, I didn't know the Gardens all that well. What struck me at once on entering was that there is an immediate sense of grandeur in the park.

This is unmistakably evident in the sight of the Main Green on the left, so heavily populated by people in every kind of multi-coloured apparel. It was like Henman Hill at Wimbledon. On my right was the Kibble Palace, a veritable glasshouse dream. It drew me at once and I pushed my way politely through the crowded main pathway towards it.

I well-remembered the almost tropical atmosphere that greeted me and the intimidating circular dome rose high above, but the mass of greenery was still immediately disarming. I walked round underneath it fully expecting, even today, elves or fairies to dart out from behind the interior forest of tree ferns and shrubs aptly arranged in one huge circle. White statues are situated all round, cleverly offsetting the greenness of it all. I particularly admired *The Two Sisters* (Martha and Mary) which I looked at while seated on a bench donated by a Mr Hugh D McLaughlan, Honorary President of the Begonia Society. I felt honoured to sit in his presidential place.

It appears that the Victorian Mr Kibble, the founder of this splendid park feature was impressed by London's Crystal Palace and arranged to have his own glasshouse at Loch Long shipped to the Gardens by barge in 1873. He was a man of some enterprise and at first used its fabulous interior as a concert hall for all kinds of events and performances. Gladstone and Disraeli were only two of the famous speakers who appeared here. The Glasgow public responded most, however, to his exhibition of photographs in dissolving light – *Hyndlandia* was one of the popular programmes shown. It was I suppose an early form of moving pictures, anticipating Glasgow's later mania for cinema.

Indeed, the Kibble Palace became a virtual Pleasure Palace but, in 1891, personal financial troubles caused Mr Kibble to sell the building to the then Glasgow Corporation. It was they who provided the funds needed to save the building for the city and for posterity by turning it into the botanical showcase it is today. I came outside again quite reluctantly. Feeling hungry for lunch, I was glad to find a tearoom at the front of a mansion house just up ahead. As far as I could see from its gateway, it was almost full, but I spotted an empty table near the back and made for it. I sat down with a bit of a bump because the chair was made of cast iron but I soon adjusted. The waitresses were more than welcoming. Soon a plate of soup with sparkling water was being enjoyed and so was the cabaret provided by a group of lightly-tanned pigeons prancing at my feet looking for crumbs. I was glad to oblige with bread provided with my soup. I didn't intend to eat all of it anyway. The bread, I mean. The soup was lovely and I was so enjoying it. I didn't notice that a lovely little girl about four or five stood nearby watching me solemnly. I gave her a piece of my bread and she smiled and threw it down among the pigeons as I watched.

'Olivia!' came a mother's voice sternly from a few tables behind me. 'Don't feed the birds with bread. It's bad for them.'

Little Olivia scuttled away immediately and I went back to my soup feeling suitably chastened and I ate the rest of my bread absently. Suddenly, little Olivia returned, still with a smile, but this time leading a little dog on a long lead. Once again, the voice called out, 'Olivia!'

The little one turned around again and left, trailing her small dog after her. Some mothers have to be listened to.

I drank more of my sparkling water and stood up, put the top on the bottle and lifted my jacket to go. I had hardly reached the little gate at the exit when another voice broke out: 'Sir!'

I turned. It wasn't Olivia's mother, but the waitress, hurrying towards me flourishing my bill.

'Sir,' she went on breathlessly, 'You haven't paid the money.'

So I hadn't. I hadn't even given it a thought. I felt very foolish. Everyone in the outdoor tea room was staring at me, including Olivia, and no doubt, her mum.

'So, sorry. I forgot.' I mumbled helplessly to the smiling waitress, and handed her a ten-pound note.

'OK,' she smiled. 'I'll get change. You wait.'

She hurried away and I sat red-faced on the nearest bench by the hedge not knowing where to look. Then, to my surprise, Olivia came slowly towards me, this time wearing a little hat but still trailing the puppy. She never gave me a glance but sat on the far end of the same bench looking at her dog. I also sat staring out, yet feeling comforted somehow. The waitress returned with my change and I made sure to give her a good tip. As I rose to leave I glanced at Olivia. She looked at me gravely as little ones do, but never said a word. I hurried away, glad to get out of the place even if it were with a bit of a red face.

As I got to its little gateway again, two middle-aged ladies, both smartly dressed and seated nearby, gave me a big smile. One of them said, with her cup to her lips,

'So you never got away with it then?'

'It was a good try' I grinned.

They laughed and I went off feeling better. That was the Glasgow way of dealing with any embarrassment. Laugh it off. They knew it, and so did I.

I came out again on to the main pathway and followed the crowd once more as they passed between the extensive Main Range botanical buildings on the right and what still looked like Henman Hill, colourfully crowded on the green space to the left. I felt very alone suddenly, being part of neither. Perhaps I should have borrowed Olivia's little dog.

Near the trees hiding the roadway there was what looked like a wedding group anxious to enjoy their wine in the sun. It was hard to believe that the busy Great Western Road was just the other side of all these celebrants enjoying a lie on the grass or a seat in the shade. I glanced around trying to take it all in. There is really so much to see here which is perhaps why there were so many people here to see it.

I didn't mind that. I don't mind being part of a crowd. I don't mind people. I love watching people. After all, I spent a lot of my acting career doing just that, watching faces. There's a story in every one, you can see it in the eyes or in the set of the mouth, in the hair-style, in every item of clothing, and in the way it's worn. Often, I don't need to talk to anyone. Who they are speaks out from every part of them, sometimes in a whisper, often in a shout. Even as we make normal lip conversations, barriers can go up, however unconsciously. Anyway, whatever the ruse attempted, I just like to look at a face, find the eyes and make up my own mind about it. I like to see them as I imagine them. Anyone's story is really everyone's story only with a change of punctuation here and there.

Years of standing in front of an audience has taught me that people in a willing mass are generally kinder than they are as individuals. Perhaps it's because in the audience collective each is free of personal restraints and can give to the moment in the company of their fellows. They are joined by their common aim – to enjoy the theatrical moment. Whatever the reason, the park is a similar kind of auditorium especially in sunny weather. There were a lot of smiles around. I found another bench further on and stopped to write up my notes so far.

To my astonishment I found I was sitting directly in front of the Begonia Section. Mr McLaughlan's ghost must have led me here. I felt very looked after. It was now a matter of deciding which path to take. There were so many options. I chose the World Rose Garden.

I couldn't have made a better choice. There is everything in this one acre of prime floral decoration carefully selected and planted, with printed information that tells one everything that needs to be known about the rose. I learnt it is an ancient flower, mainly of the Northern Hemisphere, and has been cultivated for more than 6,000 years; that there are more than 250 varieties, from the damask rose to the cabbage rose, and that the rose is used for much more than decoration. For example, it is added as a flavouring to make jam, or an ingredient in eye-drops, and of course rosehip syrup, etc. I couldn't cope with the statistics, but then I learned about the Burnet Rose, the Scots rose, and the apt Burns lyric came to mind:

> O, my love's like a red, red rose
> That's newly sprung in June.
> O, my love's like a melody
> That's sweetly played in tune...

The tune was still in my head as looked into the face of one rose and wondered why it was different from the next rose although both were ostensibly of an identical pattern.

Were our faces like that? After all we all have eyes, noses, mouths in faces that stretch from brow to chin, and ear to ear, yet we accept the fact that we are all different in some way. We take pride in our singularity, except perhaps when we have a big nose or a squint in one eye or a huge mole on one cheek – but then that's singularity, is it not?

I had to stop myself looking at roses, wondering if they looked back at us in the same way. If only we smelt as sweet. I left quickly before my thoughts got completely out of hand and I plunged happily into the nearest path thinking that there was indeed a real link between flowers and the impact of nature at its best. For instance, doesn't love itself flower? Like music in all its ranges from piano to forte, making its own kind of sound, a music for the eye as much as to the ear. I was happily musing on this when I found myself staring at a locked iron gate with a back view of very impressive houses on Kirklee Terrace. I understand the residents here have each a private key to the park gates. I had been happily meandering and musing on my way and I had no idea how I had got here. I quickly about turned and made my way back to the walkway.

This time, I disturbed a group of young actors rehearsing a play with their director on a grass sward in front of the gable wall of the houses. I stood and watched for a moment and felt nostalgic for my Old Vic times in Bristol. It was Shakespeare's *A Midsummer's*

Night's Dream which I remembered well from my playing days, but I never rehearsed it in the open air. I reluctantly left them to it and found myself again unexpectedly at the Kirklee entrance.

I retreated again and came out to walk down Addison Road and over the Halfpenny Bridge to find the Kelvin Walkway again. I was tempted to walk this but read that it led ultimately to the West Highland Way! I thought I might leave that for another time and turned again to make my way back into the Gardens. Naturally, being me, I got lost yet again and found myself at the Derby Crescent gate. As a park explorer, I was certainly no David Livingstone, but I was quite content in this green paradise to let my feet take me where they willed. Often that can be the best way, if only because, if it doesn't work out you can only blame yourself.

Oddly enough, in returning to the Gardens I found another older, more professional, company rehearsing on a proper stage built at the rear of the Main Range building while the cast looked on as they lay out casually on the overlooking hill. It was a totally relaxed scene, and Shakespeare again. I moved closer and heard one actor saying to the director, who was sitting on a chair on the grass, 'but surely if…'. It was a phrase I knew too well from my own rehearsal past and it told me I had no business being there so I moved away discreetly. Ironically, for someone who had been lost twice already, when I was asked by a lady pushing a pram how she might get to the River Kelvin I was able to tell her, having inadvertently been there so recently. I moved on with a new confidence.

I was sure I was now heading towards the main entrance again and when I passed a group of Park Rangers standing at a corner I asked them for confirmation of direction. I did so with a certain reluctance, as I told them, being a Celtic supporter, and their being Rangers.

One of them, the tallest, laughed at my heavy joke. He had recognised me, and said,

'Do you know that you went to school with my cousin?'

'What?'

'Well, so she says. St Mark's, during the war.'

'That's right. I was there for a time. What was her name?'

He told me but I had no recollection of the lady. At this point the other Rangers dispersed to go about their duties but the tall one stayed with me.

'Whit are ye doin' in the Gardens?' he asked.

I told him about my project and he went on,

'Well, did you see the Jimmy Logan plaque?'

'The what?'

'Did you ever know him?'

'Jimmy Logan. I certainly did. He was a good friend of mine.'

'Well, he's got a tree planted for him. Ye should see it. Come, I'll show ye.'

'But what about your duties?'

'You are my duty, sir,' grinned the big man. 'Come on.'

And there it was, a plaque on a small wall reading 'Glasgow Remembers Jimmy Logan – Actor and Entertainer – 1928–2001.' and behind it a flowering cherry tree. I stood and looked at it, and fondly remembered Jimmy, the man who, in 1959, asked me to play Robert Burns on his television show and, by doing so, unwittingly ruined my conventional acting career but at the same time gave me a great alternative solo life that took me around the world. Ben Allison, the Park Ranger, told me that his own son, also called Ben, was an actor too, and a good one but he was finding it hard to get work.

'Goes with the job,' I said. 'But I wish him the best of luck. There's no life like it.'

'That's whit he says tae,' Ben said wryly.

We sat talking for ages about young Ben, about life, about Glasgow, about parks until he rose up as dusk was gathering, and said.

'Come on, John I'll walk ye tae the gates. Make sure ye don't get lost again.'

'Have you the time?' He laughed.

'About ten past six!' And he laughed again. He laughed a lot, Ben Allison 'Well, thank you for giving me so much of your time, Ben.

'It's all right, John, I'll have all the time in the world soon enough. Anyway, I'll be retiring afore long.'

'Oh, when will that be?'

'Tomorrow mornin.'

And he laughed again. Then with a firm shake of my hand he

turned and was off back up the pathway. My last picture of Glasgow's Botanic Gardens is of a tall Park Ranger walking into a beautiful tree-ringed sunset.

How theatrical, but yet how many stage references this eminent Garden situation provoked, the Kibble Palace entertainments, The Jimmy Logan tree, the different companies of actors rehearsing, and this ex-actor getting lost again and again and loving every moment of it. The Botanic Gardens may be the smallest park on my walking agenda but it had a gigantic impact on me. It's amazing the power a good park has on the walker and how it gets one thinking – and feeling – about things. And people. I kept thinking about Ben's son who wanted to be an actor. I hadn't even met him but I felt I knew him. A park friend made mainly because of his father's concern. What a good man Ben senior was. I could learn much from him.

Generally speaking, the better part of us is continually looking up, though the lesser element can't keep its eyes off the ground hoping to find that lucky penny. Good people are able to find the balance in all this and live accordingly. They have a simple credo, a thing is right or wrong and that's it. They believe this completely and refuse to tie themselves up in life's complexities. The rest of us don't know what to think at times and shuffle along, thinking UP but feeling DOWN, yielding to our appetites and not to our instincts, taking the easier course in all things because to do otherwise is too much bother.

I arrived back at Byres Rd during the evening rush hour. How deafeningly loud it seemed. I stood on the pavement with hands over my ears for a few minutes before crossing at the lights. This was the smallest park on my trail yet it took the longest time to cover in the day. The Scotttish phrase is 'guid gear gangs in sma' buik' meaning that a well-made article doesn't have to be giant-sized to be effective. The Botanics is certainly effective.

In this particular park trail I met a good man who told me that his only worry was the destiny of his son and a little girl who was just starting out on the journey whose only rule was her mother. Which side will win out? Will the good man see his son achieve the success he craves? Will little Olivia grow into her own determined self, still pulling her dog behind her?

Time will tell, but then nothing is certain – except that the Botanic Gardens will still be here and, even if the Park Rangers have gone, without a doubt, there will still be roses.

Victoria Park

1912 · 66 acres

Paragon or paradox
Gentle lamb or crafty fox
Man is an animal intent on survival
And has been so since his arrival.

ANON

THE JUBILEE GATES at Victoria Park Drive North wore a coat of red as bright as the lipstick on the face of the young girl waiting just behind them. Only the gold roundel showing Queen Victoria's face and the date 1887 spoiled the metaphor, although the feminine link was valid in that the gates were funded at a cost of £100 by 'The Ladies of Partick'.

'Industria Ditat' was the inscription chiselled on the Partick Borough coat-of-arms and I gather from Steve Baker, MP for High Wycombe, that it means, 'Industry Enriches', a sentiment that I have always known as 'Work Works'. I so believe that as a writer. The best ideas come *while* you're working on a thing, not always before it. Then when you do finish the project in hand it's the re-write of the re-write that the writer looks forward to. Whichever the way of it, the words are the way and somehow they get down on the paper. The first thing they must do here is to thank the Glasgow Victorians in the Whiteinch and Partick area who had the foresight to develop this particular green site for their people's leisure and recreation.

'Industrial' is the last word I would apply to it but it must be said that the work involved resulted in totally unexpected scientific results of enormous worldwide status, but more of that anon. Walking now through the gates brings into view yet another tree-lined approach. I do love these green tunnels. This one was appealing but, in this instance, I decided instead to go rough to the right even though I was treading a path of my own making. This off-roading is a tendency of mine, I'm afraid. I saw a gap in the hedge and walked towards it, past the tennis courts. I went through the opening and found putting and bowling greens to my left well-occupied by happy families. Moving right round the square of greens I found myself at a flower-filled circle. This was very pleasant walking geometry.

I sat on a bench and took my bearings. I could see that the old football pitches were now a grassy dog walking area instead of the old-fashioned dirt surface they had been in earlier days when Scottish football was a real force. But then, neither is Scotland today what it once was. Nor was the old lady walking her old dog towards me. I don't know which was going the slower. Obviously neither was keen to play the pace-maker, but it gave her the breath to wish everyone else on the pathway a quiet 'Good mornings'.

'Good mornings' are common in the park. 'Good afternoons' are rarer and 'Good evenings' just never happen. Perhaps polite decorum declines as the day goes by. Although I did notice that whenever a young woman passed me on the pathway later, she pointedly looked at her toe-caps. Was that modesty or defence? But I still gave the top of her head a nod. It was that kind of sunny morning.

The morning was indeed good and I was just happy meantime to sit and take it all in. Victoria Park can be really beautiful in her quiet, restrained way. She doesn't push out shamelessly to grab to grab your attention but sits in her place, almost demurely, confident in her own charm and the pleasures she offers of trees and flowers on every horizon. It's rather a question of what appeals most to your own taste. I could have happily spent the rest of the morning sitting on that first seat, but I had a walk to do. It was time to get going again. But which way now?

I checked my bearings and chose to go west despite the danger of screaming, child cyclists on the pathway. One little red jacket went so far ahead his mother had to use full, operatic voice projection to have him brake. I walked on quickly ahead of him just in case he found himself suddenly in Westland Drive, but the mother had put the brake on her boy. I walked but turned away from the view I had of the roadway with its handsome terraces, particularly The Bield which stood out prominently. There are so many fine houses around this park, but a lot of traffic going both ways on all sides. It must be hard to bear such a constant drone just beyond such expensive curtains!

A small gate lay open on my left and a narrow path beckoned. I didn't know as I went in and walked over the large stones that I was stepping back whole centuries. I got the first hint in the height and sheer colour and depth of trees and foliage on either side and when stone steps appeared on my right I immediately went up. I can't resist stone steps. That's when I saw the rocks. They were staring at me as if they could see me, and I could only stare back at them. But I didn't recognise any one of them. Stone among the green is always a good combination but this had a firm beauty all its own.

What I didn't know then was that I had walked into the Quarry Knowe Rock Gardens situated in the famous fossil grove, the star feature of this park and a genuine historic-scientific phenomenon. Meantime, I enjoyed the rocks. Like Springburn, this was won from the relic of an old quarry but, unlike Springburn, the local builders, employed by the Partick Burgh Commissioners in the 1880s to clear it for a new roadway, found more than rocks. Incredibly, they unearthed the stunted stems of trees dating back beyond the dinosaur.

The *Glasgow Herald* of 14 March, 1888 reported:

> The recent discovery of fossil trees at Whiteinch... was described
> as the most remarkable that has been made in the Kingdom.

It certainly was, as I saw for myself after climbing more steps to the chalet-style Fossil House that has been built over the site. Here, under a vaulted ceiling, the 11 surviving trees, or rather, their stumps are exhibited in a protected space. I could see them clearly from the balcony approach railing. It was quite remarkable, to my eye, almost unbelievable. The fossil grove is an arboreal miracle by any standards. I felt the whole thing should be enshrined in a misty balloon somehow, but there it was under its wooden roof, a shadowy mound of soil and dusty tree stumps that dated back no less than 330 million years. These stumps were once the lycopods, or scale trees that later became club mosses, only centimetres tall but with the action of peat, rock, sand and the movement of water over unconceivable ages, they became the ancestors of the coal which fuelled Glasgow's industrial rise in the then far-forward 19th century. It was all a bit too much for my unmathematical mind but there it was, living evidence laid out now before us and under cover of a roof, a genuine pre-historic survival. And we have science's word for it.

Or rather the words of two men – John Young, the then Keeper of the Hunterian Museum in Glasgow and David Corse Glen of its Kelvinbridge Collection. They joined forces to confirm by their research the truth of these facts and establish the astonishing pre-antiquity of the find to the world. And here I was, standing on a balcony, looking down at the first evidence of this momentous evolution. It was hard to take in. I had to go and think about all this for a bit. I came out from the modest building feeling deluged by these extraordinary facts which seemed to belong to the wildest of Hollywood fiction. But it was all true.

Jurassic Park belongs to the age of the dinosaurs, but what I had just seen was 159 million years before that. I was astounded at the mathematical and scientific skill never mind the formidable knowledge shown by the scholars in the formation of this incredible bank of specific research – and then, not only that, but for it to be contained within this little house within this little park in one little district of Glasgow almost 150 years later deserves special credit to all involved. To have such a unique element in such an unostentatious site could only happen in a city like Glasgow.

I wonder how those ordinary Partick workmen felt when they unearthed those extraordinary tree stumps? What if they had just put their picks and shovels through them all? No one would ever have known. Who among them had the good sense to call the foreman then the overseer, then someone to contact the Partick Burgh Commissioner from the council before it ever got to the museum? Those first local labourers were certainly worthy of their hire. They deserve some credit for hesitating. I am captivated by the thought that an ordinary working man might have raised his sledgehammer to smash it into the first of the precious stumps discovered and something stopped him. He hesitated just for a moment and that was time for geological history to take its course. This fellow, whoever he was, was the first hero of Victoria Park. He deserves a statue if anyone does – 'To the Unknown Workman' – the small grain that precipitated the harvest. Great events often have modest beginnings. After all, James Watt's boiling kettle gave us the steam engine.

I needed to relax after taking all this is in, and coming to a wide stone at the side of the pathway I sat on it for a breather. I noticed it was provided by the pupils of the Whiteinch Primary School to celebrate the planting of a rowan tree. This fact brought me back some sense of proportion. Rising up again and walking on I was soon caught up in this park's restorative qualities.

Once again, I can only describe Victoria Park as trim and easy on the eye. She complements her neighbourhood exactly. Tidy, comfortable, but with quiet class. The calibre of the park users also indicated this social level. A red-vested runner passed me, hardly puffing at all, but then he was young. A metal bridge straddled the extensive pond and brought me on to the island. I remembered the 'inch' in Whiteinch meant island, so it was all so appropriate. The right words have a way of insinuating themselves into the right places.

In the centre stood a monument to 'The Beloved Dead of Two World Wars', surmounted by the figure of an angel looking skywards. What did all those millions of years I had just read about mean if they led in the end to such needless slaughter? Pointless killing which still goes on at the whim of the worldwide few. The world is not parks or ornaments or works of art, it's people, it's us. And all those young soldiers who were caught up in it all Yes, we *shall* remember them, even as we go about our lives, enjoying parks like Victoria, marvelling at the depths of history and biology at the fossil grove.

To cheer myself up I bought an ice cream from the nearby stall and went to take another break in the arboretum. The bench I chose was decorated with a card from a son remembering his dead father. I rose quickly. It didn't seem right somehow to be sitting there licking an ice cream cone. However, I was happy enough to do so walking round this beautiful place of flowers now lying spread out before me. Here was industry indeed, and I could see by the number of gardeners who were working and the lorries standing by, that they were still hard at it. I was especially drawn to the edging beds which displayed different flowers arranged in letters which read:

People are Glasgow, 50 Years of Working for a Just World in 1965 and Glasgow Green Year 2015.

I asked one of the gardeners if he could tell me the name of the red and blue flowers used in these floral statements. This time, I was ready for a Latin response, but all he said was, 'I hivnae a clue.' Then he mumbled something that sounded like 'Almathera and Segina'.

'Can you spell that for me, please?'

'Nae chance,' he grinned, and went back to his digging.

'Don't worry, I'll think of something.' I said, putting away my notepad.

I then headed gradually towards the exit on the upmarket Balshagray Avenue. I got there through two white tunnels on a winding trail to the mound and finally reached the No 4 bus stop at Crow Road and was glad to take a seat.

It was while sitting there I couldn't help thinking that if Victoria Park is really a young girl, then like a young girl she has a ready smile, which flowers at the slightest prompting. At the same time though, and deep within her, she contains a wider knowledge that surpasses her years and will make her, in time, the full, and realised lady that she is. I was so pleased to have met her on such a lovely sunny day. I'm glad it didn't rain. It would have seemed as if Victoria were crying.

The bus took a long time in coming, but that was lucky in a way. For I was given the chance to see and admire an entirely unexpected art work which suddenly appeared right there beside me. It was caused by the glass at the side of the bus shelter reflecting the tree next to it and the Victorian building diagonally opposite on the other side of the road. By the sheer accident of reflection, the tree's image was thrown on to the front of the house and the lovely arrangement of green on the stone and the windows growing out of it made a wonderful picture. It could have been painted by Monet, Matisse, Seurat or any of the French Masters. Then suddenly the bulk of my bus appeared in front of me and blocked it all out.

I sat back in my bus seat still full of my unexpected picture and very happy with my day. From my seat at the window I could see the tops of old tenement buildings rising into the early evening sky and, in the dreamy mood I was in, I wondered if I would ever see Vaughan Williams' lark ascending above those familiar chimney pots? Or a Sibelius swan skim over the choked drain at the back? I must be tired. I closed my eyes.

As soon as I did, I saw again, with my mind's eye, the combination of sun, shadow and light that was the fluke bus-stop painting. It held its steady image before me proving that art has as powerful an arrow as science and can pierce the heart much as the latter intrigues the brain. What a wonderful postscript reward for a walk in the park. Thank you, Victoria.

Kelvingrove Park

1852 · 85 acres

'NEVER LET A GOOD thing go to waste' is an old adage in any context but it applies neatly to Kelvingrove as it is the result of a fusion of two parks, or rather a major addition to one which indeed was in danger of going to waste in the middle 19th-century. Actually, this was the first constructed and purpose-designed green space in Glasgow and the song, 'Haste to Kelvingrove' was written to celebrate this event. A new park for Glasgow had been born. Kelvingrove did not evolve but was created as a deliberate one-off parks project by the City Council in 1852.

Sixty-six acres of land became available beside the Kelvin River and adjoining the then existing grounds known as West End Park. For almost £100,000, and assisted by the design genius of no less than Sir Thomas Paxton, this green union was to make what was called *un parc de novo*, and from the very beginning it was a huge aesthetic, if expensive, success. Despite this, many East Enders and similarly under-privileged Northerners in the city thought too much was being spent on the West Enders. It is an attitude that still prevails with some.

Appropriately, the venerable University of Glasgow looks down on the Kelvingrove twins from its high position to the north on Gilmorehill, and its towers overlook a masterly fusion of the two parks, Kelvingrove and the West End Park, with entrances at east and west. I chose to enter from the Dumbarton Road entrance opposite the Kelvin Hall so that I might come through the south-western gate where it adjoins entrances to Glasgow University and the former Western Infirmary. I did so because, for several reasons, I wanted to see the Snow Bridge at that end of the park.

First of all, it was from this bridge that Glasgow city employees dumped all the unwanted snow gathered from the streets in wintertime into the River Kelvin, which would have given an appropriate arctic look for the season. It was good to think of Glasgow snow going back into the world via the Kelvin and the Clyde. I walked along wishing that the protecting railings had been painted white to acknowledge this connection. The second reason I was interested in the bridge was possibly why the railings remained unpainted.

I read somewhere that a fellow thespian, Mark Sheridan, sadly took his own life at this same bridge in the winter of 1918. A Geordie of Scots descent, Mark was a great success in Edwardian music-hall and famous for his singing of 'I Do Like to be Beside the Seaside' early in his career. Unfortunately, in his later years, Mark's popularity faded somewhat. In a last attempt to regain his status, he wrote and presented his own show, *Gay Paree*, featuring himself and his two sons amongst a cast of 40, and directed by his wife who also managed the production. *Paree* toured to Glasgow where its creator had been a great favourite, but reviews for the first night at the Coliseum were uniformly bad and the audience was unruly. Naturally, this upset Mark greatly. He was given to depressions and the shame of this failure hit him hard. He called a rehearsal for noon next day and hurried off to the Bath Hotel. Nobody knows what happened after that.

Next day, 15 January, around 2 o'clock in the afternoon his body was found in Kelvingrove Park at the western end of the White Bridge with his own pistol lying nearby. It was deduced by the authorities that he had shot himself. But did he? The particular locale was a recognised area for homosexual soliciting, but Mark was a happily married man, not known to be homosexual. Was his body brought here by someone – or by some people? Who would want to harm such a popular figure? At the beginning of the war, his songs – especially the patriotic numbers – encouraged young men to join up, but these ditties were, by the time of Mark's death, resented by parents who had lost sons or soldiers who had lost comrades. The Powell brothers from Wales knew the same kind of reaction latterly for their immensely popular marching song, 'Pack Up Your Troubles in Your Old Kit Bag' and one of them, Felix, did indeed shoot himself with an army rifle in 1916, but he was severely distressed at the time. Suicide is not the normal reaction of actors to a poor review. The old actors always said that you're only as good as your last bad notice, but even the worst press opinion is surely not worth dying for.

Whatever the facts, it seems an extreme end for a hitherto success-ful composer-performer with a wife and family to take care for; he must have been at a very low ebb indeed. His body was taken away and later buried in Cathcart Cemetery. No one knows what really happened that morning but we know that at the end of the week, the *Gay Paree* company, with Mrs Sheridan in charge, sailed to Belfast to continue their tour. As the saying has it, 'The show must go on.' It always does.

As must life. It is a kind of show after all – the day goes by, seasons change, the years pile up and a continuity is observed if only by repetition. I had plenty of time to think of all this as I took the long walkway going east with the park falling away on my right. In a happier vein, I realised that the same snow that was once dumped into the Kelvin must have given (and still occasionally gives) the park a special attraction when it lies over its steep inclines during a white winter. On this cheerier note, I gave myself to the walk in hand which now lead me onwards and upwards towards the university rising up to my left behind a continually rising incline of green forestry. The mass of stone and concrete that housed the bell-tower of the university rose up behind the fencing. I took a seat on the next pathway bench to enjoy the fabulous view it gave me of the park below.

Behind me was nearly 900 years of learning (although the University buildings have not always been on the same spot) and they now look imperiously downhill before me, peering through the trees at the southern edge of the park, were the towers of the Kelvingrove Art Gallery and Museum. The two original parks are now held between these two iconic constructions, the University and the Art Gallery, in a pincer of green foliage that is the sum of all these years and at same time proffers a view that is timeless. I don't think I've ever seen so many trees in one place before, having only flown over the Amazon Forest, too high to observe its flora, but I understand from my reading, and from my long-held arborial enthusiasm, that the latest scientific thinking accords each one of us living in the world 452 trees each. Well, I think Glasgow's share is generous given the green appearance of Kelvingrove!

Like Glasgow itself, it is held in a ring, not of hills, but of architecture. On the Northern side is the University, on the east is Park Circus, to the south the Art Gallery and its Museum and finally on the west is the Western, waiting to become something else altogether. Together these buildings offer a safe enclosure for Kelvingrove's many park treasures. Sir Thomas Paxton, in his original design plan, took advantage of the terrain's extensive ups and downs to create a pleasure land of winding walks and flower beds, rhododendron gardens, groves and riverside walks which are a delight to the visitor. I took particular joy in rhododendrons, a favourite flower of mine.

Away down to the left at the south-east corner of the park, abutting Sauchiehall Street, are play areas, a skateboard park and tennis courts and bowling greens of Olympic standard which were updated for and utilised during the 2014 Commonwealth Games. Yet with all this in view, the park's silence was palpable. I let it wrap itself round me. Until suddenly the university bell behind and high above me rang out with such a clang that it made me jump up with a yelp which soon had me laughing. The bell tolled so loud and had such authority that I thought the Third World War had been declared. It was 12.30pm already, time to move on.

I came downhill going south-east and could now just hear the rumble of traffic in the outside world reminding me that I was in the centre of a city and not in a limitless green space, although it felt like the latter. I went down among the trees as if I were coming down a mountainside. Coming up on the facing hill I found myself watching the crowds entering the rear entrance of the Kelvingrove Art Gallery. I stood there remembering coming in through its front door with my mother when, during my early years at St Mungo's Academy. I was 13 and had won a Gold Medal for Drawing in this very building. I wondered if the drawing was still here? If so, it would be very dusty. 1943 is a long time ago.

The museum really is a superb building, a palace of art in every respect. It rules the whole area it overlooks; the queen of structures. A mighty edifice, it well deserves the popularity it has as an arts venue and museum since its very beginnings. Kelvingrove, both park and gallery, has housed no less than three prestigious International Art Exhibitions, in 1888, 1900 and again in 1911 when the Scottish National Exhibition came to the West End of Glasgow. The Gallery itself was, in fact, built from the proceeds of the park-based 1888 Exhibition and many more followed in the years after. It has certainly earned its keep.

This early connection with art is probably why there are more statues in Kelvingrove than in any other park in Glasgow. The elaborate and popular Stewart Memorial Fountain is certainly prominent, being an 1872 memorial to a former Lord Provost, Robert Stewart of Murdiestoun, who, despite vehement political protests, was responsible for bringing the pure water of Loch Katrine to Glasgow in Victorian times. It is still a running asset to the city. The statue collection includes many to other eminent men of high merit: Lord Lister, in passive mood in his stone seat and Lord Kelvin, sitting on his chair within its circle of grass, pen in hand and book on knee. There are so many Kelvins in the area. The park itself, the river, the bridge, the district, Kelvinside, Kelvindale and Kelvin Hall, opposite on Dumbarton Road. His Lordship may have been named for any of them, or they from him, but he remained, at heart, plain William Thomson, born in Belfast in 1884 with the brilliant mind that made him a world authority on physics and telegraphic engineering. In a long career, he was constantly invited to teach at other universities but he remained loyal to his adopted Glasgow, dying at Largs in 1907 aged 83, a rich man and deservedly full of honours.

Author Thomas Carlyle, on the other hand, is given the privilege of only his surname on his memorial stone. He might not have approved, as he appears to be trying to struggle out of its concrete pillar. There is also, on the other side of the park, a formidable reconstruction of a black lioness with her cubs, an artefact given to his native city, by one John S Kennedy of New York which I misread, with some confusion, as John F Kennedy. I am sure many do.

For me, however, the most impressive memorial in the park is that to a professional soldier, Lord Roberts of Kandahar, Pretoria and Waterford, VC, KG, KP, GCB, OM, GCSI, GCIE. His Lordship, another Irishman by the way, must be the most decorated soldier in history. He certainly enjoyed a long life, dying while visiting troops in France at the start of the First World War. He looks every inch a Field Marshal as he sits astride his horse at the eastern park entrance looking imperiously over Kelvingrove's many fields. Behind him lie the architectural perfections of Park Circus and its surroundings, a building area on a par, architecturally at least, with the University and the Art Gallery.

They provide just the right urban backdrop for the park. Looking out over the greens and trees from the east, I couldn't help thinking that Kelvingrove is certainly worth its status as a milestone in city landscaping. She's feminine, too – despite all the military show – the haughty big sister of our Glasgow parks. She looks good, in any weather, and has the authority that belongs to real class and pedigree. It is often overlooked that Kelvingrove is twinned, but her brother park couldn't be less like her. The former West End Park attached is spare and male with a trim haircut as opposed to Kelvin's flowing locks, but they make a good pair. This is an ingenious spacial coupling that has won for the township no less than eight Green Park awards. The two parks are divided, or joined, by Kelvin Way, a wide walkway taking motor traffic coming up from Sauchiehall Street. But roadways were beyond my remit, so I turned left up the park section of the road thinking again of the huge debt we owe today to those Victorian park-makers.

I halted in front of the newly-restored bandstand, a small, charming relic from another age advertising *A Trip Through the Twenties* as its latest attraction. It was like a little doll's house set against a tree background. It sports wooden benches at the front of its raised platform and concrete slabs for the rest of the auditorium; it has a foot in all audience seating camps, from mid-Victorian to Roman. At least, this is a park amenity that has survived, and good luck to it.

And then, the bell for 1pm. It might have been signalling lunch (which I had brought with me) but the sound of the bell also seemed to ring through the park as an anthem to past military deeds, a tribute to war fatalities, hence the plethora of memorials throughout the grounds. Memorials include tributes to soldiers of the Highland Light Infantry (Glasgow's own regiment), to the Cameronians and to airmen of the 602 Glasgow Squadron. There is also a memorial to Battle of Normandy veterans but nothing, as far as I could see, to sailors and men of the Merchant Navy, nor of the Home Guard, the Fire Service and the ARP. Still, if we had to add all victims of wars, all of us would be included in one way or another. The helpless, spectator citizens – men, women and children, who were lost in the Blitz, all lost loved ones or family. War casualties despite themselves. That's the terrible pity of it. After a moment's silence to myself as I stood by the statue of the Boer War soldier I gladly returned to my topic in hand, the park.

This time I took the top way from over the bridge and retraced my steps towards the belt of trees. En route, I passed a council van parked in the shade of the tree. I noticed the driver was asleep at the wheel with a smile on his face. He was obviously enjoying his lunch break in the sun. I tiptoed past and went down an incline drawn by another kind of stone carving I could see straight ahead of me. There was something familiar about it. I looked at the base, and sure enough, there was the name, 'Benno Schotz'. It was my old friend, Benno, a Glasgow Estonian who was, in fact, the Queen's Sculptor. He made a bust of me as Robert Burns in 1979. It is now in the Scottish National Museum in Edinburgh. Well, at least, it's in the store room of the Museum. I've never seen it shown. I have the happiest memories of Benno, not only in the sittings, but at our Glasgow Art Club lunches. He was a lovely man to talk with, especially about himself. This was not conceit, nor ego. This was his artist's way of full expression in everything. Now here I was standing looking at his *Psalmist* and remembering those great days of wine and chat at the lunch table.

I turned away to sit on the bench facing the work. I just wanted to look and remember. As I took my place, I saw that the bench was dedicated to the memory of Dr Tom Honeyman. I knew him, too, in my student days. What was going on here? I was in a public park between two names that were very important Glasgow connections to me at one time. Dr Tom is the man most famous for purchasing the Salvador Dali masterpiece, *St John on the Cross* for Glasgow for permanent showing in the Kelvingrove Gallery less than a hundred yards away. He who also joined with Dr Mavor (or James Bridie, the playwright), and the Cosmo cinema owner, George Singleton to found the Glasgow Citizens' Theatre 70 years ago. A theatre that is right at my acting roots. I felt privileged to have known such talents as all these men were. Suddenly, I wanted a glass of wine in my hand again and the sound of Schubert in my ears, but all I could hear were the strains of James Bridie's chirpy, glee, 'West End Perk', which is hardly in the same class, is it?

I don't know how long I sat there but I suddenly noticed a spider on my jacket. I shook it off. Why couldn't it have been a butterfly? A butterfly would have been so right for such a special moment. Eventually, I forced myself to get up and take my place in the queue of people walking along the riverside. It was amazing to hear the sound and see the power of the Kelvin. This was no slumbering stream but a near-thundering river. I realised now why the snow was poured out into such a vigorous water machine. It's very refreshing indeed to walk briskly by running water. I tried my best to be brisk as I could under the curtain of trees on my right. Every second walker ahead of me, most of them women, seemed to have a dog. I wasn't sure who was walking whom.

At one point my way was barred by a trio of push-chairs coming towards me – three women, all talking at once. They were so engrossed they never even noticed I was there. I had to nip quickly to the side into the bushes to get out of their way. I suddenly remembered that at the other end of the park there was a tree called the Suffrage Oak in honour of the women in Scotland who fought so bravely for the vote. Thinking of what that took in terms of prison years and lives lost one can only admire them. I have no doubt today's women would show the same spirit. So they can edge me off the path any time they like.

I was on track again to return to the Snow Bridge where I had started the day. I took my time. I was reluctant to end my afternoon under the trees. Eventually I had to come out again onto Dumbarton Road. Now I was at the bus stop and facing the Kelvin Hall. It reminded me of yet another famous Glasgow name, the late Sir Alexander Gibson who conducted the Scottish National Orchestra there so many times. I knew him in much earlier days when he was the accompanist at the Citizens' Theatre when Andy Stewart and I had to sing a duet in a play called *Right Royal* We called him Alec. His was my kind of music. Not the kind that fills the Hydro with screaming youngsters but the sort of sound the makes you catch a breath, brush back a tear or stand up and cheer. Glasgow did it for me with the Orpheus Choir in the old St Andrew's Hall and with thousands of male voices at Celtic Park singing 'The Fields of Athenry'. Or any pipe band anywhere playing 'Highland Wedding'. It's all in how one hears things and if they touch the heart. The sound of any young child's voice can do it. The simple fact is that if you give to music, it will give back to you. So I repaid the compliment to Kelvingrove by walking back along Sauchiehall Street singing quietly to myself, 'Oh, I do like to be beside the Seaside...

Bellahouston Park

1895 · 175 acres

IN THE SPRING OF 1988, Graham Roxburgh, a successful, English-born Glasgow resident, was running, not walking, through Bella-houston Park when he had an idea. A former RAF officer, Mr Roxburgh was, and is still, a trained consultant engineer with an architectural background and a long-held admiration for Charles Rennie Mackintosh. It was, therefore, no surprise that his great idea, between strides, was to see the former's House for an Art Lover built on the very grass he (Graham) was running through at that moment. Situated as it was on the site of the old Ibroxhill House on the Dumbrek Road side of the park, it seemed to Graham that the space was ready and waiting for something to be built on it. At that time, Glasgow had just been nominated Euro-pean City of Culture and it, too, was looking for an idea to mark this award. Graham Roxburgh had come up with just the thing.

In December 1900 Mackintosh, under the name of Der Vogel had been invited to submit plans for a '*Haus Eines Kunstfreundes*' (House for an Art Lover) in a Europe-wide competition for archi-tects promoted by Alexander Koch at Darmstadt. Toshie won the Special Purchase Prize of 600 marks but his building plans were never put into fruition. Graham knew this, and with the experience of developing Craigie House (his own home) he set about selling his idea to the powers that be in Glasgow. At first, it was dismissed as implausible, but he persisted, and two years later, the building, as Mackintosh had imagined it, was standing in its Scottish home, and not in Germany.

It was a magnificent feat all round, and full credit must be accorded Mr Roxburgh, for it can be said that for a park still famous for its 1936 International Exhibition and several outstanding Papal Masses, Bella (as locals refer to Bellahouston Park) is increasingly being known for the living art work that is House for an Art Lover. The house now rivals all of the existing worthy amenities in the park, including the Palace of Art Centre for Sports Excellence, The Glasgow Ski Centre, Leisure Centre, a sculpture centre, Cycle Centre, Pitch and Putting Course, Hockey Pitch and even the Papal Garden. An all this is within walking distance of Ibrox Stadium, the home of Rangers FC (only Glaswegians will know the irony of this latter pairing.) Yet such is the spaciousness and generosity of parkland in Bellahouston that it never for a moment feels cramped or crowded. It is a magnificent conglomeration of place and effect. Bella – Houston. It is literally just that, beautiful Houston.

I thought of this as I sat in the all-white basement of the House for an Art Lover among the happily chattering ladies seated in couples before the crescent Mackintosh windows which looked out on every kind of flower imaginable. Had it been a lived-in house no doubt this would have been a dark cellar or space for a carriage, but as it is it is a delightful restaurant. I could have spent the whole day in the House and in its music room but I knew I must get out and about before the threatening rain came down, although I wouldn't mind being trapped among all these great-to-see Mackintosh attractions.

The first thing that came in sight on my exit was the Glasgow Ski Centre, made out of the steep hill ahead and with a whole line of schoolchildren on the skyline waiting to descend. I got out of the way quickly in case they landed on top of me. I moved along the roadway to the right heading for the Palace of Art but thinking what a very good idea to have a properly organised skiing centre in a hilly city park. Once again, the utilising of assets. Good for Glasgow. I duly arrived in front of the Palace of Art alongside Paisley Road West and stood before it admiring its classical Art Deco black and white frontage.

This building is the last remaining evidence of the famous 1938 Empire Exhibition which drew 12 million people to the park yet still made a loss. The exhibition was especially known for its Tower of Empire, or Tait's Tower, after the architect who designed it. It stood on top of Ibroxhill overlooking the contrasting clachan, or highland village, among the trees. It displayed its markedly modern tower top for all of stark and hungry pre-war Glasgow to see and wonder at. The working-class in the city at that time had only the cinema and football to take their minds off being out of work labouring hard for pennies. A general urban depression lay over the whole city, so this tower was a challenge and a change, to say the least. The Tower and the Palace of Art, by the way, were the only two Exhibition buildings intended to be permanent. What a pity that later short-sighted war-time strategies insisted that the Tower be demolished. It would still look modern today.

In fact, what a great idea it would be to rebuild the Tower on its original site and make it available to the citizens and the world once again. Why not? What a wonderful addition it would be to the contemporary Glasgow which is evolving so splendidly around us now. And it would also serve as a much overdue honour to the architect who designed it. Thomas S Tait is virtually a forgotten man today. Yet he had a worldwide reputation in his time. The Sydney Harbour Bridge and St Andrew's House, Edinburgh, were just two of his previous projects. Lord Elgin was behind the hiring of the talented Tait and gave him the opportunity to initiate a whole village of modern buildings in beautiful surroundings and with a vitality which defied its supposedly temporary creation. Had a war not occurred who knows how the art of architecture might have advanced in Scotland. It was a Mackintosh situation once again. Tait was so ahead of his time that he was held to be a failure in his own city and so was left to find fame in exile. A very Scottish story.

The Bellahouston Exhibition was deemed a huge success and received rave press, but it was allowed to pass, and its main treasures were lost to posterity. Thanks to Tait, however, and his team of young architects, colour had been returned to a grey city, and how it needed it 77 years ago. Real excitement, only found on the football field in Glasgow, was restored when Celtic won the Exhibition Cup at Ibrox beating Everton in the final. Yet art was given its place with this exhibition of so many fine pieces in such stimulating surroundings. I have an early memory of travelling to Bellahouston on a tram-car to see it all. As Primary School pupils we went from Parkhead in a 'caur' as we called it then. I remember the occasion particularly, because my Uncle Jimmy McNamee was the tram conductor!

Now, all these years later, I am standing in the same park gazing at what was once the Palace of Art, something that was brand new at that time, except that now the Art in its title applies to the art of sport. I couldn't help but be a little disappointed. I went in, looked vaguely around and thought, 'this is not my scene'. Mr Bruce, the Duty Manager, reminded me that today fitness is an art. I took his word for it and, thanking him for his time, left by the imposing main door, wishing the building was still a Palace of Art in the old fashioned sense.

Although the weather was still showery I gulped in the damp air with relief and resumed my walk by the side of the hockey pitches, watching through the railings as Paisley Road West dealt with its traffic. Then suddenly the sun came out. It was so bright I had to put on my sunglasses. It was then I noticed a very odd sight. Coming towards me along the same path was a lady leading the largest dog I had ever seen. It had legs like an elephant and I looked for a way to get off the pathway. However, when they drew slightly nearer, I saw it was a tall man walking with his much smaller wife! What had misled me was that he was wearing a green jersey and a brown hat and with his head down he merged exactly with the background of forestry behind him so that he became, or appeared to become, a pair of disassociated legs which I mistook for a dog. Such is the trickery of the natural setting when the sun is in the right place

I walked on trying not to look too far ahead, took one of the paths to the left and came across the stone cairn commemorating the first official visit of the newly crowned King George VI and Queen Elizabeth to Glasgow in 1937. I gather this was the first official act of their reign. Turning further into the trees and climbing upwards I came to the sunken garden behind its gates. This was the site of the original Dumbreck House bought by the trader Moses Stephen in 1850. He changed the name to Bellahouston, which became the title of the park when it passed into the responsibility of the City Council in 1895.

The main interest here at the top of the park are the 16 concrete slabs called 'The Glasgow Roots' on the top of which are chiselled various aspects of Glasgow life such as the Barras, Tenement Windows, a Cobbled Square, a floral patch, a plea to save the Glasgow Savings Bank, even a collection of electric light bulbs, amongst many more carved references to the city that surrounds us. Although this urban proximity is, as usual in all of these parks, increasingly hard to believe as I continue to walk through what is to me total countryside, such is the press of trees, bushes and plants over acres and acres of tumbling grass and rambling dogs pursued by breathless owners. One thing I did notice was that all the dog-walkers were young. Perhaps they had to be, pursuing their charges over those huge layers of sloping green that sit between the pathways.

By this time, I was down in the lower ground by the Leisure Centre and was very impressed by the full car park. Bellahouston obviously makes good allowance for leisure as pleasure. I continued along by the extensive pitch and putting course which would have flattered any normal golf course. A golf course has been here since 1899 only three years after the park itself opened. This place really is space generous. Two skyscrapers have a privileged, if distant view of it all. A better aspect is shared by the bedroom windows of the many little cottages that mark this particular boundary. They are lucky tenants who can wake up to this scene each morning.

These same tenants would have been aware of another park occasion that was even bigger than the 1938 Exhibition. This was the visit of Pope John Paul II to Glasgow in 1982 and the park was the scene of a special Mass on a ceremonial platform which still remains. Two-hundred and eighty thousand people attended that day and nearly as many again when, years later, Pope Benedict followed suit with Archbishop Mario Conti and celebrated Mass in the open air. Sir James MacMillan wrote a special John Newman Mass for the occasion and over 700 singers were in the choir. Television cameras from all over the world were present that day and it was estimated that the audience exceeded a billion.

In 2011, a Papal Memorial Garden was built to commemorate these momentous events, not only for the park, but for Glasgow as a whole. I approached the now empty site with a kind of reverence, and I could have sworn a halo was hanging over the whole area. Perhaps that was just my innate Catholic bias – or was it something that was really left in the air? If so, it was in tears, because it started to rain!

The rain was gentle at first, but gradually it increased until it was bucketing down. And I didn't have my travelling umbrella. I just gave in to the elements and treated the rain like a face-wash, as one must in Glasgow. This may also have made my long walk back to the Dumbreck Gates seem longer but the tall trees either side gave me a kind of shelter and it became more like a steady tread down the aisle of a large roofless cathedral. The trees seemed to kiss each other above my head and little could be seen either side. Soon the rain really began to make its impact and I could feel the increasing need of shelter.

Then suddenly ahead of me was an unexpected sight in such weather. A line of schoolchildren of all sizes stood spread across the roadway listening to a young man who must have been their sports teacher. He shouted and stepped aside and the whole crowd of them came dashing towards me. About a dozen healthy pupils of different shapes and sizes running full out and getting nearer by the second. It was like a battle charge as they shouted and screamed. I wondered if I should kneel down and let them jump over me? Or should I try to jump over them? I did neither but moved smartly to the right among the bushes as they raced past me. I watched with mouth wide open. Here were young people in a downpour rushing past me yelling their heads off. It was exhilarating to see young life in school uniform going hell for leather down a tarmac pathway.

Yes, that's what it was – exhilarating. This whole park experience has been that. I had to remind myself that this area, too, was a hub park for the 2014 Commonwealth Games – and small wonder. It had everything – space, expanse and character. Not to mention every possible sporting amenity. How could the Games have succeeded as they did without the help of so many Glasgow Parks? I gave the thumbs up to the sports teacher as I passed.

I headed speedily for the gates. I was soaked to the skin but was decidedly content. I had been to a very special place. I had seen the beauty of Toshie's House for an Art Lover, enjoyed the nobility of the Palace of Art, and felt the ghost of Tait's tower tapering into the darkening sky. As I walked the last long hill after the rain, I was sure that a Sign of the Cross had been lightly indented on the grass. All I knew for certain was that today in Bellhouston I had been re-baptised by rainwater. Quite honestly, I felt I had been blessed.

There is something in this park's atmosphere I hadn't met in a park before. It has what I can only call a rural solemnity. Of course, it may have been due only to these two mammoth papal occasions, and I personally understood this well. But I felt it was more than this – something to do with the loss of Tait's Tower to bone-headed, wartime caution. The side-effect was the professional martyrdom of Tait himself by the inability of his generation, apart from Lord Elgin, to see what he was trying to do. The Mackintosh parallel is uncanny. Toshie is now of course, an icon. Tait may not be in the same bracket but today I felt his spirit was with me in the park, mourning the loss of his masterpiece. Had it been saved, who knows, Mr Tait might have become a Mackintosh.

I came out of the gates soaking and solemn, but glad I had done the day. I had first seen Bellahouston when I was in primary school, and now I had returned as a pensioner and the effect the park had on me today, spiritually at least, was to remind me that I hadn't really changed a bit. Thank the Lord. I came out on to the road again, gratefully muttering my own made-up, and often improvised morning prayer, that I say, not with palms together, but with fingers crossed:

Let me work in you today, Lord, as you work in me,
Let me live in you as you live in me.
Let me remain in you, as you remain in me.
Keep me in you spirit, Lord,
For with it, I can do anything,
Without it, I can do nothing.
Without it, I AM nothing

Pollok Country Park

1967 · 361 acres

Nor Clyde's own course
An ampler prospect yields
Of spacious plains and well-improven fields

JOHN WILSON

THESE FEW LINES from Mr Wilson's 18th century homage, 'Clyde' ideally introduce this extensive park; the prospects are indeed ample, as one can see from the start. Pollok Country Park is the largest acreage of land ever gifted to the city by a benefactor, and within its generous acreage there is everything any park walker might need – orienteering tracks, sheltered lanes by running water, the mandatory pond, not to mention cycle lanes and athletic tracks. Animals abound, from butterflies to grey squirrels that sit up and beg with front paws bent before them. And then of course there are the two buildings which are the stars of the Pollok show – Pollok House and the internationally-acclaimed Burrell Collection. Indeed, the story of this particular grand park might be, as we shall see, the tale of two houses!

However, at this moment, I was certainly made aware of length and breadth of my chosen park from the start of today's perambulation. It was even a decent ten-minute walk from the Pollokshaws Road entrance at the White Cart Bridge to the formal entry at a stone gateway some way in. As I stood there, even the front gate looked daunting. I wondered if I should have brought my passport. But shaking off the feeling of intimidation, I dutifully took my turn in line after a long crocodile of chattering children going the same way and went forward without any hesitation, with a whole trail of couples queueing up behind me. Something was obviously drawing us all on that lovely sunny Sunday morning.

So far there was no sign of the 'little pools' from which the name 'Pollok' derives. These acres we were all tramping go back a long way. The waterways were vital to the earliest Bronze Age settlers who came to this area in pre-Roman times. The Romans themselves arrived around 150 AD to add their contribution, and the Levern, Brock and Cart rivers did their bit to create what later became farming country. They also give their names to current streets in modern Pollok and the large housing schemes that surround the park perimeters.

Medieval times saw most of the land fall into the domain of

Walter, the hereditary Great Steward of Scotland, and thereafter followed the usual family course which inevitably led to the Maxwell family's taking over the present park lands when George Maxwell was knighted by Charles I for services rendered. The Maxwell family home was named Pollok House and it survives today as one of the park's main attractions. But the pathway I was now walking would lead me soon to that other star of the park – the Burrell Collection.

I ambled through an enchanting forest-like way which cleared to reveal, on a broad green sweep, the first stop of the morning – a modern building of such quality that it makes an immediate impact. The Burrell features a facade of red brick with white ornamentation and glass – lots of glass. This morning it was absolutely surrounded by people. Bring on the sun and it brings out the people. I hurried through the crowds to the main entrance, then forward through the foyer and into the first exhibition space to find Rodin's *Thinker* sitting deep in stony thought. I was so astounded to meet a classic item so soon I almost didn't know what to think, but it certainly got me off to good start. The problem was where to go from there. There is just so much to see at the Burrell Collection.

The purpose-built museum space is undoubtedly one of the most iconic buildings in Glasgow. It was designed by a young team of Cambridge architectural talent and houses under its archways and in its many corridors an almost embarrassing treasure trove of art works and artefacts, furniture, statuary, busts, broadswords, canvasses, dishware of every possible style and a wealth of domestic implements and furniture as well as historic flags, banners and coats of arms. Almost a superfluity of choice to the visitor. There is also a restaurant on the ground floor available in case it all gets too much for the visitor.

I was immediately drawn to the rear of the building with its glass wall looking out to a forest of trees. What a clever contrast it is, the accumulation of priceless art works on the inside, each piece demanding attention, and outside an unadorned, natural green wall looking in, making its own silent comment. It also allows the viewer to enjoy the ever-present world outside while having the mass material and occasional masterpiece available in the interior. It is a cunning mix and helps give a needful sense of proportion.

It would take the rest of this book to do justice to what the Burrell Collection is in each of its different sections. Suffice to say, if the visitor goes round each of the levels he or she will be rewarded by a real awareness of how art and its off-shoots have developed over the centuries, seeing it realised in almost every shape, form, line and material. Some of the artefacts are quite exceptional and other pieces quite ordinary, but the sheer mass cannot be anything but impressive. It really has to be seen to be believed and unlikely as it might seem, the entire collection is the work of one man.

For me, the question that began to nag at me as I walked through it all was, is this a mere temple of cupidity, or is it an expression of one man's genuine enthusiasm for other people's artistic skill with brush, needle or chisel? What I really wanted to know was not the history of each artefact and *how* it came to be but *why* Sir William collected it all in the first place.

His family business was shipping, run by William and his brother George following the early death of their father, but I noticed there was only one ship on view, the SS *Strathclyde* which, ironically, was sunk during the First World War. Everything else here, the thousands of objects – more than 9,000 in fact – were once the sole property of one man who added to it continuously throughout his life because he couldn't stop himself. It was his sole enthusiasm, his passion, this collecting bug, and some might even label it his mania. Burrell always had an eye for a bargain in whatever area, and he could not resist the lure of a profit, however modest.

On the other hand, the amassing of such wealth was a mighty achievement for a Glasgow boy who left school at 14 to join the family business. But young Willie Burrell had the money touch without doubt, making canny decisions in times of economic downturn. Burrell was one of the lucky few, like Andrew Carnegie, who once they got an idea could turn it before long into a money machine. Driving a hard bargain becomes a way of life and the sole aim was to profit by consistent application to the idea in hand. Total energy was given to the specific intent.

This can be more than an obsession. For the true enthusiast it becomes a natural way of working, and the super-rich successes take the mindset almost for granted. Nor do they have the least moral scruple about it. They have no need of justification, it is just how things are done, and tycoons do so with unbelievable energy. Carnegie did it with steel, as Burrell with shipping. They bought in buyers markets and sold when the economy recovered until they had so much money they didn't know what to do with it. Carnegie built libraries and founded charities, Burrell bought 'stuff', and here it was, or most of it, all around me. The quality is amazing but the quantity is almost overwhelming. I could hardly take it all in and stopped taking notes, so intimidating was the prospect of annotating everything.

Though I might have scruples about Burrell's collecting motives, I have none at all about the building that houses the collection. It is a formidable but admirable architectural creation, fully serving the purpose for which it was created, that is to show of bits and pieces, large and small. It is hard to think that the Collection proper began with the sale of shipping stock to the Admiralty by the Burrell brothers in 1914 and the buying back of same at a profit in 1919. Having established the precedent, they did the same at the start of the Second World War in 1939 allowing the spate of miscellaneous purchases to go on. But here Burrell met with a minor set-back. He had moved at this time to Edinburgh and even he was beginning to see that his collection was outgrowing him.

He decided, therefore, to donate what he now called The Sir William and Lady Constance Burrell Collection to Edinburgh, but a further snag arose. There being a war on by this time, Edinburgh Council took it upon themselves to possess the surrounding iron railings on the Burrell home 'for the war effort'. This was a phrase, despite its patriotic basis, used by many to cover unashamed plundering on a huge scale, but every council in every city in Britain was only doing its national duty as conditions demanded. Melted-down railings meant more guns, so they had to go. Burrell was so furious that he went as well – back to Glasgow – and he took his Collection with him and in 1941, almost pettily, signed it over to Glasgow City Council.

That's the sort of man he was, decisions were often made on impulse. For the most part, he profited, but occasionally, the boy in him prevailed. The problem now was, where were they to put it all? According to his will, he made it a condition of the gift that the collection was to be sited 'away from the poor, soggy air of

Glasgow' which made it difficult for the Council to find a place to put it. It took until 1967 to realise Burrell's wishes, when eventually Pollok House and its estate became available, thanks to the generosity of the Maxwell family. Lady Burrell must have been relieved to be able to move around again in her new home, Hutton Castle on the Borders.

Even Burrell could see that he could not cart all this 'stuff' around with him indefinitely. He was no fool, far from it, which is why he had decided to put it all in responsible hands while he was fit enough to do so. The accumulator had become the benefactor, even if he was motivated by the realization that, in the end, he couldn't take it with him. The monster collection found a fitting home indeed and the design of Burrell House was put in the hands of the young architects at Cambridge. The result was a contemporary structure that is now recognised worldwide as an architectural icon, and the name Burrell was thus handed down into history.

Now, at the time of writing, the Burrell Collection is about to be made more accessible with a council-backed renovation and remodel which will begin later in the year and stretch to 2020. The exhibits will, unfortunately, be closed for much of this time, but the collection will be better displayed and more secure when it remerges. In the meantime, a selection of Burrell's pieces will be on show at Kelvingrove Museum; perfect excuse for a day out at Kelvingrove Park and the chance of a game of lawn bowls after taking in the collection amassed by Sir William. How totally unexpected is the fame he has found in his posterity.

Sir William Burrell was a Glasgow man of many opposites with a good eye for a bargain, but I am quite sure he never guessed that his natural and unconstrained lust for artefacts would make him immortal – if only for the fact that he was the reason that a now world-recognised Glasgow icon was built on this idyllic park space. The city of Glasgow councillors certainly benefited in becoming owners of the building and its contents, especially as it can now be seen in a splendid park setting just as Burrell stipulated.

I now could only gawp endlessly at one man's wealth of possessions. Yet it was hard to see Burrell himself as a mere buyer and seller of battleships and teaspoons. He was perhaps two persons in one, good and bad, greedy yet generous, with a kind of cloaked kindness that can co-exist with a wilful ruthlessness. His instinct for accumulation might have been solely driven by a tremendous energy but it was also assisted by a good eye that helped him to a real understanding of art and artists. He knew they had to sell to live, so he bought and sold and they benefited. So did we. In the long run, as with most things, whatever we do, it all works out one way or another.

I wanted to know more about the enigmatic man, and I found it written on a wall upstairs. I learned that he was born at No 3, Scotia Street in Glasgow. A mundane start. He was introduced to art by his mother, who was a collector herself, with a genuine love of art and artists. Young William caught the bug and he never recovered. Hence his fascination with artistic works of every kind which led him, with the same application that made his a success-ful business, to set out to learn as much about creative culture as he could. In this he was helped by another Glaswegian, Alexander Reid, whose gallery was near the Burrell office in George Square. Reid had sponsored Van Gogh, so he knew what collecting was all about. Reid was a mild man. Burrell was not. He fought with anyone who ever opposed him, especially at auctions, but Burrell-had his own maxim, 'I like to understand what I have if I can.'

And understand Burrell certainly did, from the moment he bought his first painting, a modest portrait of the 18th century British school, purchased in 1890. And from then on, the arts tide never ebbed, culminating in the purchase of a Frans Hals in 1948 for £4,500. He had his own aesthetic taste. He admired restraint in painting and works of elegance. He was also generous to Scottish artists of the Glasgow School, particularly the work of William Crawhall, but he couldn't draw a straight line himself. Not that it mattered. As he said,

'It's not the Collector, it's the Collection that matters'. That says it all. Typically, he began to keep a purchase book in 1911, into which every item in the growing Collection was scrupulously recorded.

Meantime, he had married and had a daughter, and was knighted by King George V in 1927 and, besides the increasing art interest, he somehow continued to run a successful shipping firm until life itself caught up with him and eventually added him to its own collection when, in 1958, he died at Hutton Castle.

I left the building with thoughts about Sir William Burrell and came back out into the afternoon sun. It took the hairy cows in the field to shake off my continuing Burrell preoccupations. But I was fully distracted when I learned from a notice on their field fence that these same docile park creatures produce more dung annually than an African elephant! I was duly impressed but left it at that, moving quickly on towards that other house in the park – Pollok House.

What a change from the Burrell's modernity to walk through a beautiful arch into a lovely early Victorian home, still obviously of its period. As is shown by the way it welcomes one with shadows and soft light, stairs going up and down and an almost library atmosphere. Small wonder it is an ideal setting for recitals of classical music. This restrained and polite tone was also evident in the manner of Angus Lyons' greeting to people as they came in. His trained BBC background was still clear in his confident delivery and relaxed tone. I was at ease at once. We had a pleasant conversation about the contrast between the Burrell's mammoth impressiveness and the Pollok's gentle welcome.

I went downstairs to the restaurant and ordered a glass of wine with my late lunch. I was walking, not driving. As I sipped contentedly I was glad I had come here today by bus rather than driving. I couldn't help thinking of what a dear New Zealand friend had once said to me, 'Drinking when driving is not recommended as there is a great danger of spilling the wine.' The babble of conversation around me was a surprise, but it was the noise of people happily engaged and relaxed and it helped to make me so. I was glad to follow their chatty example with the two ladies at my table. Nothing of importance was said but that, as Robert Louis Stevenson reminds us, is how it should be: 'Only trivia should be discussed at mealtimes.'

It was then I noticed an attractive blonde lady of middle years taking copious pictures of the huge iron grate that was inset on the tiled wall behind our table. It was a wall-length cast iron construction made by Finlay and Son of Glasgow in the heyday of Glasgow's engineering prowess, when iron was almost an art form in the city. This piece of metal was a first-rate specimen, decorated with copper-coloured pots and pans and kettles. I spoke to the photographer to find that she had ad been intrigued by the contrast the domestic implements made with the dark, shadowed grate, hence her need to capture the scene on film. I told her that at one time, every house in Glasgow had the same sort of coal-fired grate with oven and later gas rings, only our tenement grates were much smaller and perhaps held only a couple of pots and a kettle.

'Oh, I would have loved to have lived in such a house,' said the charming photographer.

'No you wouldn't,' I thought. But I said nothing.

I bid a polite farewell to my table companions and went back indoors and along the corridor to the book-shop – another location always irresistible to me. There I met Aileen Reimer, who was in charge. I commended her on her obvious energy. She told me she got it from her customers.

'Everybody has a story in them,' she said, 'and I get it out of them at the counter. I just love it. It keeps me going, you know.'

Wise woman. I made my excuses to leave, saying I would look at the books upstairs. 'You'll not read much up there. The books are behind bars.'

Sure enough the books in the big library on the first floor are behind a protective wire netting but it didn't spoil things for me. I just sat back in an armchair and took it all in happily. I couldn't help thinking how different the atmosphere here was compared to the dense and crowded richness of the Burrell. This was still the Maxwell family home and that quiet cosiness was almost reassuring. Stuff doesn't make for ease and home comfort. Money can buy most things but it can't buy atmosphere. That is something a place earns over the years, over whole centuries. That's what is enticing about ancient ruins, though Pollok House is certainly nothing of the kind. However, with its dark wood and tiles it has atmosphere in abundance.

Then it came to mind again that this is the biggest park in Glasgow and I yet had 5 kilometres of walkways still to pursue. I took a deep breath and plodded on doggedly but contentedly through Pollok's hoard of natural amenities, enjoying a variety of the green serenade from all sides. My legs were beginning to feel it a bit, but what is the body after all but a machine. I quickly switched it on again and continued on my way – ignoring stone steps that lead into forest glades, roads that were meant for mountain bikes, playgrounds for toddlers and pensioners, football pitches, rugby fields, a field for horses as well as for cows, and at the end an abutting golf course of professional standing and real class at Hagg's Hill corner.

John Betjeman would have loved all this. He was an Englishman at the forefront of the green rebellion and in the '50s he was already into the benefits of the simpler pleasures freely available in life. He wrote:

> One cannot assess in terms of cash or exports and imports an imponderable thing like the turn of a lane, or an inn, or a church tower, or a familiar skyline.

That is so true. The important element is often the unexpected as in the sight of rippling water, bold rocks or a sweep of grass and this expansive park proves it. It could be said that Pollok had everything, from the overwhelming to the understated and this could not be better exemplified in the two building it boasts, the Burrell Collection and Pollok House. Perhaps in the end Pollok Country Park is indeed a tale of two houses.

What the Dickens is there left to say about it?

Nothing. So I let a little rhymed sequence which suddenly began to shuffle around in my brain. I let it gradually form as I walked the long path to the road exit in the calming atmosphere of a delicious dusk which, as you know, I like to think of as twilight.

This is what it came out as:

I love twilight
That world of half-light
That's neither night nor day.
It's the way
That shadows play among themselves
Like children in the dying day.
In a delicate, dancing sway

Making pictures of every shape and size
Of things we never see with open eyes.
What a lovely way to rehearse for night's sky
By way of a holy light
And all sound muted in a sigh...

Dusk was giving way to the dark, and I was merely a shadow on the pathway surrounded by common growths, like that tree, that particular bush, those different flowers. I was charmed by the way that the fading light played among them all, creating shadows that made still more delightful pictures. The shadow is an under-rated artistic tool. Its presence it highlights the colouration in anything and brings into relief the essential outline of the picture presented. But the core is always there, even if undefined.

After all, everything depends on how we look at it and each pair of eyes does its own thing when confronted with an image. It's called independence by some but it can also be a truculent self-assertion. Which is often why complete accord in anything is hard to achieve. We can't help our own bias and pre-disposition. We're only human. But it is this which too often determines our initial focus. We have to look hard to see an alternative perspective.

Modern thinking appears to have ceded all appreciation of nature to science but I can't see why a super-knowledge of quarks, black holes and the rest can't help one to appreciate the cheeky assertion of a tree branch over a moss-covered wall, or the sweep of hill by a running stream, the sturdiness of a tender flower, or the sheer impertinence of a squirrel. All these things are seen every day in any park at some time in the day, and understood by all. Deliberate entertainment of any kind is often nothing more than distraction, but the pleasures of the park, served as they are by the seasons, are there as a ready antidote to most of the self-imposed stresses we all know at some time.

Whether to move house or not, to change the car, replace the washing machine, there's always some decision pending, some choice to make about something or other. All I can say is that these sort of things take on a less vibrant, urgent tone when considered while walking through a park. Whatever we decide about our appliances and our lives, the grass will continue to grow, the leaves will fall every autumn, snow will go on laying down its white carpet. Love, like anger, is an emotion fired by neurons in the body. The hormones involved can be charted appropriately, but how can a sigh be charted, or a sudden leap of the heart? Yet these thing can happen in a park by turning a corner and seeing a view, catching the scent of roses seeing a bird swoop into its tree. We imbibe a respect for nature and all natural things and this makes us feel good. In short, parks are good medicine.

All this and more tumbled around in my head as I stood looking back on the patch of country side I had just left. By the mere fluke of positioning, at the Golf Club there was no building in view, neither Pollok House nor the Burrell, only the green sweep going south and carrying with it a verdant simplicity in its unity, a reassuring certainty in its precision and wide perspectives. This is what a park should be. A green park in all it variety should carry us with it into wilderness, and transfer to our senses a comforting permanence and peace. At this point of the walk, I felt I had the whole world to myself. I was in a rare, deep quiet and wanted only to relish it. I had found, if only for a few moments, what can only be called the desert of myself. A basic place free of the jungle I kept making of the Eden I had somehow lost in the cluster of things to do. One can be too busy.

Queen's Park

1862 · 148 acres

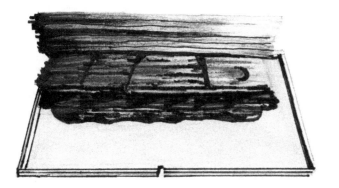

As part of our SHIELDHALL TUNNEL PROJECT we will be establishing a site compound within the park near the Victoria Road entrance. This work is due to start on 31 August and will be in place until the Spring of 2017. We will also be carrying out consolidation work across the park from this site to the duck-pond at Pollokshaws Road until early 2016.

Some pathways may be closed during this work.

ON EXACTLY THE fine summer morning that I was due to walk round my Park No 11 for this book, the printed notice above appeared on the railings near the main gate. It was from Scottish Water: There was no apology or appeal for permission or co-operation. There it was, an order, abrupt and to the point and that was that. I moved along to the entrance at Victoria Road and had a look. It was as if an army had invaded the park. Trucks, vans, cars crowded the main drive and a regiment of men in yellow jackets scurried here and there trailing wires, ropes and various implements while the sound of an electric saw split the air. Suddenly, a tree fell. The first casualty of the attack. I was aghast, and seeing this a helmeted gentleman standing nearby laughed and said, 'Don't worry sir, new trees'll be planted.'

'I'll not see them.'

'But somebody will.' He grinned at his riposte, and I had to agree.

'True enough,' I said, hardly believing what I was seeing, until I couldn't stand the noise and seeming confusion any longer. The considerable work force seemed to know what they were doing and why they were doing it so I left them to it and walked away, closing my ears to the carnage. How very sad that the park will have a huge length of its circuit cut off until 2017. But it is the price we pay for progress, but I couldn't help but wonder what was 'strategic' about Shieldhall. They had enough equipment assembled around the site to drain water out of the Sahara so I assumed they knew what was required for Shieldhall.

I tried to get my mind reorganised for the walk of the day even though I would have to omit a neat chunk of pathway and traverse the rest by means of temporary signposts. It was not at all what I expected, but that's part of the adventure I suppose, dealing with the unexpected. I decided on an alternative start at the recreation ground which is not officially part of Queen's Park but only a road's width away from its southern rim. Since I had lost a park portion to the Water Board I could make it up by adding the 'Rec' to my walk. In any case, it's a favourite morning dog-walk area for the neighbourhood animal lovers. And sure enough, there they were in their huddles talking animatedly while the dogs stood by patiently, or sniffed patiently at each other, while their owners caught up with the day's gossip. I couldn't help thinking what if the dogs barked among themselves and the owners sniffed each other? No, maybe not!

I left them to it. It makes one think that dog-walkers come to the park for the talk rather than the walk. What they might not have known as they chatted was that they were standing on the very turf where history was made, right here on this same wide open space, its two levels divided by a tarmac pathway clearly seen behind the neat iron fencing. I'm referring to that other Queen's Park of course, Britain's only amateur football team in the professional league. Queen's began playing on this very ground when football came to Scotland as an amateur pastime sometime around the middle of the 19th century.

Although the Scottish Football Association wasn't founded officially until 1873, the ancient sport had been formalised in England a decade earlier when J.C.Tring, a cricketer, set down the rules improvised by students at Cambridge a decade before. Tring's rules for what he called 'the simplest game' were officially recognised by the new Football Association in 1863 and printed in all the national newspapers. Consequently, football spread throughout Glasgow like a non-fatal plague until there were more football clubs formed in the streets of Glasgow than there were in at the time in the world. And it all started from here, the recreation ground at Queen's Park.

Football was quickly recognised as the poor man's game, as opposed to rugby which was accepted as the sport for the better-off. Glasgow in particular took up footie, or soccer as the Cambridge students had called it, and soon every second street seemed to have a football team. This was especially true for Irish immigrants from nearby Gilmorehill. They were watched by the middle-class boys from the nearby Protestant churches, mostly Highlanders, who had previously been more interested in shinty and tossing the caber. But it was these well-to-do Highlanders who were now attracted to the new sport and they improvised matches among themselves almost immediately. This led to games like bachelors versus married men and smokers versus non-smokers, until the tenement boys also took up the game with enthusiasm, before long playing it regularly and playing it well. However, it was the toff boys who were the first to get organised. In 1867, they formed a team which became the Queen's Park Football Club – a strictly amateur organisation, as all football was then, and Queen's Park, to its great credit, still is.

From the start the team was successful and even took their skills to England where they met English teams like Notts County and the famous Corinthians of much longer standing – and beat them! These games were restricted however, because the Glasgow men had to get time off from their various offices and pay their own train fares and accommodation. Meantime, the poorer boys too were going ahead in their own way, creating rough and ready teams representing their districts, even their streets, with names that showed their vigour and diversity – Glasgow Thistle, Cowlairs and Lugar Boswell etc.

An army team was next, the Third Lanarkshire Volunteers. These military sportsmen were based just across Cathcart Rd from Queen's Park and were later pillars of the new professional Scottish Football League as Third Lanark. Indeed, it could be safely said that around this time there were more recognised football clubs that is, with definite rules, names, and colours (even if it were only a scarf) in any city in Britain. The game had hardly got out of England, yet here in good old Glasgow, the poor man's game flourished like no other. And it all started in this park. Yet no one seems to be aware of this unique historical and sociocultural fact. I do wish there were some formal marking, like a football pitch laid out in this section of the park so that this site might underscore its legitimate claim to a place in Glasgow history. A sign on the Queen's Avenue railings should read 'SCOTTISH FOOTBALL BEGAN HERE circa 1862.' The very year Sir Joseph

Paxton's Queen's Park next door was completed. To my mind, it is pertinent to the park theme here, that football has such a prominent place in this chapter, since the Queen's Park is Park No 11 in my writing order – and there are 11 players in a football team!

Also, in my opinion, the fact that the adjacent space made itself readily available for the new football craze is as much relevant to the park as the Battle of Langside, or the annual visit here of Zippo's Circus or even the utility the space offers as a spare parking lot for Hampden's National Stadium just over the hill. Hampden, by the way, is the present home of Queen's Park FC and also houses the premises of the popular Scottish Football Hall of Fame under its Director, Richard McBrearty. It is an iconic site linked with its own history, but Scottish Football needs to remember its roots lie in the proletariat when the game wasn't the province of agents and foreign investors and clubs whose only concern now appears to be solely to rear boys cheaply to become players whom they can then sell for millions. This is sport as a trade not a sport. Players used to be signed in order to develop as good sportsmen not as properties for profit.

However, one man in Scotland, who still has the right idea for the sport is David Duke, a Govan man and founder of Street Soccer (Scotland). A talented player himself he took part in the Homeless World Cup in Sweden in 2004 and this gave him his idea of founding a new level of football for underprivileged boys. In 2009, he founded Street Soccer to give young lads something to do, something to aim at and in much the same way that football itself grew in the city, his organization flourished. Today, it has spread all over Scotland thereby justifying his philosophy, 'Give people hope and you can give them a future.'

David Duke deserves to be given these very recreation acres as his own base, a properly organised football ground where games might be played on a regular basis even under the name of the old prestigious Third Lanark Volunteers which was so sadly lost by callous malinvestment, proving again how big money has totally devalued modern football as a sport. It would be more than apt if football might be formally linked with this playing area, where it was Glasgow-born nearly a hundred years ago. With this thought in mind I made my way across Langside Road. I gave myself up to

A WALK IN THE PARK

the long climb from there up to the flagpole. I passed the old Path-head farm buildings now the Park Offices. I thought it said 'Park-head Farm' on my guide, then I remembered we had no farms in Parkhead, only a farm milk cart on weekday mornings. You bought double milk on the Saturdays. I crossed the main prome-nade, a wide pathway intersection which was well-peopled for the time of day. Then I realised that some of them were walking to work or to another bus route and using the park as a shortcut south-west to get from Victoria Road to Langside Road. Parks have their practical uses as well.

Crossing to the north side of the pathway I noticed two trees with placards before them. The thin tree was called the Halabjy Tree, so-called because it was planted to honour the Kurdistanis who were killed in the chemical bombing of Halabjy by Iraqi extremists in 1988. Passing the same point recently I noticed that the tree had been uprooted. By whom? And why? The much thicker trunk still stands. It belonged to the tree planted in 1970 to mark the 25th anniversary of the founding of the United Nations. How wonderful that these events should be recorded so fittingly with trees in a corner of a Glasgow park.

I finally got to the flagpole and was glad to take a breather on one of the surrounding benches and take stock. It was a fine day and the weather allowed me a wide view all round. I must say I was gobsmacked. I was 209ft above the ground and facing due north at sea level. Small wonder this was a look-out post from time immemorial, although it was raised even further to create this wonderful flagpole viewpoint. The walk up certainly has its rewards. All round me Glasgow was laid out like a carpet for my own special viewing.

There was the University of Glasgow, defiantly staring me in the face. Every kind of dwelling was visible, from pretty cottages to the traditional tenement, rich and poor, rising skyscrapers, chimneys of all sizes, and above all, those piercing church spires. I had a full panorama, nothing hidden from view. I walked round the circle of benches taking in the familiar hills, the Kilpatricks, the Campsies, Cathkin Braes, Arran and Ben Lomond and its surrounding hills, or rather mountains, further off in the distance,

The flagpole itself carries no flag. It doesn't need to, its colours are all round it and about it, below in the park. Green upon green. Green for the 'G' in Glasgow, every shade, shape and density of it can be seed even beyond the wide, sloping hillside. The view was exhilarating. I felt like jumping over the fence and letting myself roll down the inviting brae towards the trees. Instead, I came down from the heights and was soon lost among the trees, an experience I always enjoy. I emerged on to what looked like a ring of rough boulders, all big and some huge.

This must be the site which local legend says dates back to the Iron Age – more than 30,000 years – before the Picts and Romans. Be that as it may, the stones certainly did look old. They were ringed round the ashes of a fire and the empty beer cans that obviously dated from as long back as the previous night. 'Touch a boulder and grow older' is the saying that occurred to me but I didn't, instead kicking an empty curry packet out of the way, I walked through the long grass on the winding downward foot-made path that led me to the main walkway which circles the park.

I was stopped suddenly by the sight of one little daisy staring up at me from ground level – one tiny, little flower, its yellow face ringed by its white circlet all alone within the huge area of grass. I laughed out loud at the impudence of this pretty little thing. There it was, hardly an inch out of the ground but, once again, proof of Nature's ability to make its statement anywhere. This mini-example was worth a whole truck-load of empty beer cans or any amount of used curry packets. Much reassured, I carried on until I reached the edge of the green, there on the corner was Camphill House.

This was the original park mansion, now flats with separate garages, but still possessing that classical, Early-Victorian look. Hearing shouts and yells I knew I was at the five-a-side football pitches. More football. I was at the opposite end of the park from the original football pitch but you can't get away from football in Glasgow. The volume and ferocity of this handful of five-a-side players sounded more like the Battle of Langside than a friendly soccer exchange, but that's Glasgow too. If a thing is worth doing, it's worth doing loudly.

Mention of Langside reminds me why the park has its name. It was first planned as 'The South Side Park' but it found its present title when the full history of Langside was uncovered. The Queen concerned is not Elizabeth or Victoria, but Mary, Queen of Scots, a true Stewart, daughter of King James V, who, when he was on his deathbed, wryly foretold that his crown had *cam wi' a lass, an wad gang wi 'a lass*. Then he turned his head to the wall and died. The first lass mentioned was Margaret Tudor, the daughter of Henry VII of England, who married James II of Scotland, thus giving the Stewart house a legitimate claim to Elizabeth's throne, hence the latter's deep hostility to Mary. Her royal father had not been far wrong. His daughter had an ominous start to her regal life. Her childhood saw her exiled to France and brought up as a French Catholic princess who, for purely political, Franco-Scots reasons, when both were children, married Francis, heir to the French throne, and became Queen of France. When she was widowed soon after in 1561, she chose then to return to her native Scotland.

She was young, beautiful and clever and staunchly of the Church of Rome. She was not welcomed home by the Protestant reformers. Consequently, she was to know a brief four years of reign as the Scottish queen. In a sense, Mary was a victim of her time. She was as rightful a monarch as her cousin Elizabeth was dubious; a king's daughter indeed but illegitimate via Anne Boleyn. Actually, Mary Stewart was also the legitimate Queen of England, but this was strongly disputed by the wily Good Queen Bess.

Mary, on the contrary, was ingenuous. She made many errors in her reign but with the help of her half-brother, James, Earl of Moray, she persevered at court and was encouraged by the love received from her own circle. However, matters weren't helped when, all too hastily, she married young Lord Darnley. He was later murdered, it is thought by the Earl of Bothwell, whom, to everyone's astonishment, Mary then hurriedly wed.

This so shocked the Earl of Moray that he led a rebellion of the nobles in 1567 which forced Mary's abdication in favour of her infant son, with Moray acting as Regent and virtual ruler of Scotland. Mary was imprisoned at Loch Leven but escaped to Dumbarton Castle where friends like the Duke of Hamilton came to her support. Moray challenged the Duke at Langside (on the southern edge of Queen's Park) and a fierce battle resulted at the top of what is now Battlefield Road. Moray won the day, and

Mary, who had watched from Cathcart Hill, made yet another mistake by fleeing to England and seeking the expected refuge with her cousin Queen Elizabeth.

Instead, after a much prolonged imprisonment, she was executed 20 years later, in 1587, cruelly beheaded by royal mandate. Tradition has it that Mary's pet dog ran out from the folds of her skirt as she knelt at the block. There is no doubt that her beheading was seen as a kind of martyrdom and she became, and to many still remains, a tragic Scottish heroine. Mary came to her end like a true Queen, almost as if she were relieved to meet that destiny which was to die bravely in a foreign land on the order of one who shared her blood. One who some might also say, usurped her birth right to the English throne, but at least, in her posterity, Queen Mary of Scotland got her reward at last in having a splendid Glasgow park named for her. I can't help thinking it ought to have been called the Queen Mary Park.

Mary Stewart never became an old lady but she represents the Scottish woman of this area, who have that classy spirit. The breed is evident yet even if it's only in the brigade of doughty ladies who live in style in the mansion-like tenements that surround a park named for a Scottish royal. This prestige is evident in the quality of the buildings in Balmoral and Royal Crescents running alongside the recreation ground and also in the converted Crosshill Church in Queen's Drive as well as homes seen in the nearby Queen Mary Street. As the names might suggest, there is no lack of architectural majesty in most of the housing that rings this high-grade park.

I decided to go right from Camphill House down to where the bridge over the burn used to be and the path led me down through the trees to the boating pond. The boathouse still stands and men and boys still push out their model boats into the water but the ducks and swans seem to hold greater sway these days despite a prominent notice which reads 'Please do not feed the ducks', an injunction regularly ignored by the lines of parents and children throwing bread onto the water. The Council may indeed have a point in trying to prevent the rise in vermin, particularly rats, but the children don't listen. And what parent can refuse a child a crumb at a duck pond?

I continued by way of slightly uphill gradients and gently falling slopes, which brought me back to the road between the swings and bowling green on my left and the old bandstand on my right. The latter has recently been modernised but it's now more of a concrete stand with no hope of a band. Pity. But even nostalgic relics must move with the times. And that applies to me as well. I now realised that the only lack this lovely Paxton park has – TOILETS. This was the reason I headed for the Glasshouse on the Hill. One of the best amenities in the park, this 1905 building with its imposing gates more than lives up to its majestic site. It is the starting point of the Queen's Park Trail, and one can see why. Everything stems out from here. The original Glasshouse was demolished in 1930 but the steps remain at the bottom of Camp Hill. It was on them that John MacLean, a schoolteacher pacifist and genuine local Red Clydeside hero, was photographed in 1918 as the first Soviet Consul in Britain. He was later imprisoned in Edinburgh for his left-wing views, but precisely because of that he still remains a figure of great respect in Glasgow.

I was now able to enjoy the many fine assets under glass, although I wasn't sure of the fish tank, which seemed to have every possible species of fish swimming in never-ending circles trying to find space for themselves. All the same, it was an undeniable water spectacle. It called for a coffee in the restaurant which I similarly enjoyed from the comfort of a couch.

Completely revived, it was then the turn of the dome area and its shop before exploring the reptile house which, admirable as it was, was not to my taste and my stay there was short.

Significantly, the place was crowded, so I was very much in the minority.

I came out through the picnic area and made my way down towards Langside Halls at the Shawlands Cross end of the park. This ex-city centre bank was moved here in 1902 because it was recognised as 'one of the most beautiful banking houses in the city.' Small wonder it soon settled as one of the cornerstones of the new Queen's Park. Now it flourishes as a centre for every kind of local event. I moved from it to find my way to next park glory, the Scottish Poetry Rose Garden.

The garden was formerly the walled garden linked to the original Camphill Hothouse but in recent times a rose garden was created in the space and the special theme given was Scottish poets, from 15th century Robert Henryson to Violet Jacob of the 20th via Robert Burns of the 18th. The Gaelic Poet, Sorley McLean is also honoured here, as well as a man I appeared with in my time, Hugh MacDiarmid. His real name was Christopher Grieve. He and I read in Kirkcaldy Library at one time and we enjoyed a drink afterwards at the local hotel. It was good to remember this while looking at his Little White Rose of Scotland in the very centre stone of the ground. He would have been delighted at its placing. He deserved it. He could be a stern little man, but his was a singular, Scottish poetic voice.

The exit path took me on to the grand staircase which was a very elegant route to the main gate past the bowling greens and tennis courts and towards the continuing war noises of the construction gang who were now putting a big white fence around their whole area. They couldn't hide the pride of the park which rose up all round their utilitarian screens like a green God outraged. It was good to see this natural triumph. Even if, just to the left, other trees and bushes hid the one scar which temporarily blemished the Queen's lovely face. This was the murder of a young English girl by a dope-maddened man who left her body among these same bushes high on a hill above the old bandstand. A simple stone marks the spot today with her Christian name painted on it – 'Moira'. She will not be forgotten.

My last thought as I left through the main gates of Queen's Park was of that lovely, lost park slogan – 'This Park is open from dawn till dusk'. Yet nobody thinks of what can happen between that dusk and its dawn. Yes, indeed, 'It cam wi' a lass an' it'll gang wi' a lass'. Our today was the tomorrow they never saw but we can still remember their yesterday which was why, on Sunday, 24 October 2015, Glasgow organised what they called 'Moira's Run' in which people were invited to run, walk, or stumble around Queen's Park in honour of Moira Jones, with all proceeds going to charity. Good for Glasgow! And may Moira rest in peace.

Rouken Glen Park

1906 · 227 acres

We can walk where we like, when we like and as far as we like,
but, unfortunately, we can't walk away from ourselves.

ANON

I FLEW INTO GLASGOW recently from Berlin on what aircrew call
the 'hair dryer', that is, a plane that still has the old propeller
blades on the wings rather than the modern jet mouths. I found
myself looking down on the Giffnock, Newton Mearns and
Thornliebank districts of my own city and being quite astonished
at how green they all looked. It was park-time, twilight – the end of
the day – but the great parkland of Rouken Glen, my 12th and final
park, seemed to rise up to meet us as we began the long descent into
Glasgow airport. How proud I felt that green growth still has a
place among that welter of housing and supermarkets, roadways
and railways, telegraph poles and big, skinny wind turbines.

As I went through the gates of Rouken Glen Park the next
morning, a big, black bird flew overhead, all alone with the whole
sky to itself it flew with no apparent effort but with complete
serenity and assurance. It stopped me in my tracks as I looked up
and watched it make a large circle in the air as if it were checking
out the place – or was it my place in it? I hesitated before moving
on in case it swooped down on me. This was a real king of birds.
It was wonderful to watch. Its ease in the air told me that it knew
where it was and what it was doing and why it was doing it and
nobody dare intrude while it did so. Only the crick in my neck
stopped me following its progress. I wasn't here for the air show
but for my last park parade.

Rouken Glen is unique. It is its own master among parks because
it's an outsider. It is different because, as I was to find, it isn't a
park, it's an experience. No two parks are alike of course, and each
is its own experience but, even at first glance, Rouken Glen is
different. The whole day ahead of me was to prove as long and
fascinating a diversion as any walk in any park ought to be. I headed
first for the visitors' centre as I thought it was the sensible place to
start. It might give me some idea of what I'm in for. However, the
first building I came across was the garden centre. As always, I find
such places almost extraneous in a park when there is shrubbery

and flowers all around, but I suppose it is helpful for those who want to carry away specimens for home and garden.

Standing at the entrance way, it was the building behind that caught my eye. So, denying myself a plant-shopping opportunity I walked round to the rear and encountered a series of miniature football pitches made for five-a-side football matches. You just can't escape football in Glasgow. However, this set-up was slightly different in that it was occupied by miniature players of primary age, girls and boys, shouting loudly and playing happily with no great sense of rules but with every evidence of enjoyment. I watched for a bit through the railings then walked on until I found my way barred by trees. It was then the trouble started.

I thought it a simple matter just to find my way through them to the path I guessed was on the other side, but the obstacle became a barrier of thorny bushes that prevented my reaching the just-visible rear path. I made to go forward to check my options, but next thing I was checked myself by the bushes. In no time I was thoroughly entangled and completely imprisoned in nettles and spiky branches. I felt very stupid and pulled myself away only to find my path blocked by a metal post embedded a foot away from a tall wire fence. I tried to squeeze through between post and fence but couldn't. I dragged off my jacket and tried again but still couldn't budge. All of a sudden, in a single, stupid moment I found I was absolutely stuck between metal post and fence!

The sound of the children shouting was still in my ears but my throat was becoming increasingly dry with panic. This was unreal. I took a deep breath to calm myself. Everything, in any situation, is in how you breathe. I muttered a quiet oath to myself, feeling a right fool in the undergrowth but tried to remain calm. Right, I am stuck. What do I do now? I quickly took another deep breath. I realised I was too thick-chested to wriggle through. I had to become thinner. Off came my pullover. Right. Another deep in breath but the pressure worsened. I closed my eyes. As soon as I did so, my body seemed to slump, but it actually moved a little. My heart leaped, and a fervent prayer came to my lips. Encouraged, but still slow I very gradually I eased myself an inch to the left. Pause. Then another inch. Then – suddenly – I was free. I gave a loud shout and carrying my clothes got out of that damned thicket as fast as I could.

I have never been more aware of my own ridiculous frailty than I was during the five or so minutes I was pinned behind that post. It was like seeing greenery with teeth, or at least long finger-nails. I was almost hysterical with the sheer relief of being free again although now sweating badly. I certainly wouldn't try to take a shortcut again. I hurriedly dressed. The children on the other side of the fence were still playing their game not realising that a real chump of an adult was giving himself a hard time among the thorns. Luckily, nothing was torn and only my dignity suffered, but only I knew that. I brushed the leaves off on my jacket and tried to pull myself together but I was still shaking a little. Oddly enough, as I made my way out of the bushes I found a football stuck in the branches just as I had been. I pulled it out quickly and gave it such a hefty drop kick it must have gone all the way across Scotland to Murrayfield! I moved on and at last I was back on the main path where I ought to have been in the first place. I turned right and walked on trying to forget the whole embarrassing incident. I now saw I was at the gate of something called the Enterprise Academy. As I stood there, an oldish workman came out of the gates and as he approached, I stopped and asked what the Enterprise Academy was for?

'Fur young yins who don't know whit they want tae dae in life, run by them that don't know whit they're dain' eether.' Then he laughed, 'Naw, I'm only jokin'. It's wan o' they initiative places,'

'I know what you mean.'

'It's mair than I dae. Whit are ye dae'in in the park?'

'I'm writing a book about–'

'Here,' he interrupted, ' Ye're no wan o' they politicians ur ye?'

I laughed, 'God forbid.'

'You don't sound Glesca.'

I shrugged and quickly asked him, 'Can you tell me which path I ought to take?'

'It depends on whoar ye want tae go.'

'It doesn't matter really.'

'Then why bother askin'?'

'I just thought that –'

'It doesnae maitter whoar ye go in the Glen, ye ay come back tae whoar ye startit. Juist foally yer feet. Aw the best.'

And he was off before I could say another word. He left me standing there. I felt as if I were Alice in Wonderland and had just met the Cheshire Cat! I shrugged and followed my own feet as directed.

Turning right again I was suddenly in my own kind of wonderland. It was another tunnel of trees, but this one was different. This was the woodland walk, and it was like balm after my sticky start. The surroundings were so thick it was almost dark. The foliage was positively dense, but I went on fearlessly simply because I was free to move. It was dynamic. The path then twisted and went down and suddenly I was going over a wooden bridge only an outstretched arm away from a gushing weir that caused the water below my feet to swirl like a whirlpool. I was looking at white energy personified.

But it was sluggish compared to the waterfall which I met in the forest a few minutes further on, and yet another wooden bridge upwards as I made the ascent towards the main park again. I did so reluctantly. I loved this green underworld suggested by the rushing water. I could have stayed here all day. As I moved off, the noise made by the stream was like traffic of a new kind. A noise in the mind somehow. I wondered at the great power it suggested. I have stood behind the Niagara Falls in Canada and watched it as it fell, but this noise from a dwarf fall in a Glasgow public park was almost on a par in its intensity. Size doesn't matter when real power is involved.

I stood there watching and shouted above the noise in my excitement. A man passed by paying no attention to me or the fall of water, but then, he was having trouble with his dog. Although I wasn't on a lead, I felt I, too, had to be pulled away. I moved away reluctantly until I found I was now walking alongside the boating pond, with yet more trees at its centre. It was extremely relieving be at peace again with the comfort of such a lovely view. The static waterway didn't have the semi-oceanic look of Hogganfield Loch but it was impressive nonetheless. There were no boats, no ducks, no people so I carried on in my solitary way down the path until it turned me away to the left and pointed me towards the visitors' centre again. I headed over the grass towards it.

I love walking on grass. There's something daring about it, for in my schooldays it was a criminal offence to walk on the grass in parks. I'm glad we now have grass freedom – otherwise a piercing whistle would have made me jump. Funnily enough, I only heard recently, during a weekend in London, that it's still an offence to walk on the grass in Paris. *C'est stupide, n'est-ce pas?*

The quiet of the visitors' centre was just right. I gladly tiptoed around the information boards trying to take it all in. Like Victoria Park, Rouken Glen has links with that pre-ancient Scotland which nudged the Equator. This was markedly noticeable in the rocks which I had seen when coming out of the Woodland Walk. It is also evident in the Giffnock Sandstone which is used today in so many of the posh houses surrounding the Glen. Little do these householders know that they are faint echoes of the Carboniferous Age, as are the rock layers they call Orchard Beds. All this is stated and effectively illustrated on the walls. I really enjoyed the library-like stillness as I made my tour around this captivating space.

What impressed me most however, was the Celtic Capelrig Cross which was found while they were developing the park in the first decade of the 20th century. It was held to be more than 1,000 years old. I think its ancient image might have been the reason for the stony silence in the room. There is so much to see here at the centre that is interesting, like details of something they call eco-drama where plants are given a theatrical life, as it were, through music, movement and multi-sensory storytelling. I should like to have seen more of this but 'performances' are at special times. It's a primary school project, the wider intentions of which began when pupils turned their school playground into a garden. Good for them.

I learned too, that the Auldhouse Burn which runs through the park is the fastest moving waterway in Glasgow, and it all began 300 million years ago. I wonder that I left it so late but I came out feeling rested, refreshed, edified and informed. However, although I had no idea of it, an even better source of learning was waiting for me up at the gate. The rain had come down again and I wondered if I should go back to the visitor's centre, but then, as happens in Glasgow, it went off as suddenly as it had come on, so I took off my cap, shook the rain off it and carried on to the main exit. And here I was given another unexpected addition to this remarkable, incident-packed day.

As I approached the park gates I noticed on the window of the park house before them a sign: PARK RANGERS. Just as I did so, a personable, middle-aged lady in what looked like genteel overalls came out of the doorway. I pointed to the sign and couldn't resist calling out jocularly to her.

'Is that the local football team?'

To my surprise, she answered quite haughtily and immediately, 'No, it is not. I loathe and detest football.'

'I'm sorry–' I began but she carried on –

'This is the Park Rangers House and I am a Ranger myself.'

'Oh?'

But as she said identified herself she smiled, and it was the smile that did it. It showed her better-class Glasgow confidence and her natural disposition to engage with other people. Like so many of my fellow-citizens, she did so with complete honesty. It was the trademark generosity and sense of hospitality that most Glaswegians share, but I had the feeling she would always speak her mind, this one. Not in a mannered, English way but in a school-teacher-like Scottish way, as if she were addressing a class. She began to do so with me. I had tried to soften things by saying, 'I think you may be the only Woman Ranger in Glasgow. The Lone Ranger?' I grinned, but she waved me to silence.

'A little obvious don't you think?'

I pouted slightly but said nothing. The 'Lone Ranger' went on:

'It matters little. So, what have you been doing in the park?'

I told her. 'Good for you,' she continued 'About time somebody wrote the book on our parks. I was thinking about doing so myself one day. '

'So you should, but let me get mine out first.' She laughed.

'Go ahead. And now if you'll excuse me, I'll get on with my job.'

And with that she sauntered off down the hill towards her waiting van.

It was a brief exchange but a telling one for, in an impulse, it sent me back the short distance to the visitors' centre where I took the opportunity to look up, a little more thoroughly, the history of this remarkable park. As I read it occurred to me that it was almost worth a book in itself.

Apparently, it all started here in the latter part of the 18th century with the Auldhouse Burn and the Crum brothers. They were millers and enterprising with it. They knew the value of the burn here especially in the pace it had coming off the waterfall. They approached the owner of the surrounding land, a gentleman by the name of Montgomery who owned most of Ayrshire at the time and had crept up northwards enough to own most of this wee quarter in the south west of Glasgow. The Crums pressed Montgomery to sell it to them and he did so. In no time, the go-ahead brothers had a mill built by the burn before you could blink. It was so successful, that before long they had 12 meal mills up and running. That's how the park got its name from the original 'Rock-End-Mill' which the Glasgow accent was soon converted to Rouken and the Glen was added in due course.

Eventually the Crums sold out the whole area to Lord Rowallan as he became, and in 1904, for reasons of his own, he gave it to Glasgow as a gift to its people and it became a public park two years later. Glasgow had plenty of parks already but they accepted it and made a lot of improvements, but it proved too expensive to maintain and they were happy to close it at the outbreak of the Great War in 1914. It was then taken over by the army as a training ground and after that the Glen took a long time to recover. Lots of amenities were lost through deterioration and disrepair. Things just drifted on although the park space was still popular with the Glasgow people for school day trips and week-end excursions. It was a readily available rural alternative, but, lacking direct planning control or adequate funding things were allowed to drift disgracefully. So much so that in 1984, Glasgow City Council decided to cut its losses and rent the whole park to Eastwood District Council on a 125-year lease, and it is they who still run it today.

They have done so with such effect that Rouken Glen is now in the top ten most visited parks in Scotland. This is a high mark of park status and is one totally deserved by the Eastwood authorities. One can see it in the care given the walkways and general amenities but also in the way in which the Glen's ancient natural assets have been left to speak for themselves in the woodland walks and high gradients. This is the best of both worlds in a carefully preserved continuity. This is why people flock to enjoy Rouken Glen. It is so much itself and doesn't care who knows it.

I stood at the gates and thought that it was quite funny that all this green splendour sprang from a couple of Crums!

Sorry, I couldn't resist that, but it was indeed they who showed the required drive and initiative and had sufficient faith in their own vision to hansel running water for industrial purposes. And in doing so, set in motion a process that would ultimately result in a park space of majestic proportions.

It was strange how I seemed to see faces in everything as the shape of things above and around me changed in the shifting light. I heard voices in the wind coming at me from every direction. I was undoubtedly tired. My park walks had been a demanding project physically but rewarding mentally and spiritually. I discovered that the religious layer to the city lies deep, and the parks have an unworldly air about them at times. That, of course, is only my personal opinion, but then religion is a truly private matter, or should be.

I stood at the gates and had a long, last look back hoping I might see my big black bird again. Not a sign. The sky was empty. The birds were already home and was my winged welcomer already in its nest in some corner of this amazing conglomeration of fields? What else was living snugly among the many branches or under the blanket of various greens that stretched all the way to the horizon. The mills have gone, but their work was done. The military stamp has been eradicated. So many changes yet the glen still encloses that vital, hurtling stream, the Auldhouse Burn. Rouken Glen as a natural resource is almost back to how it looked to our forefathers. The difference is that Montgomery's land is now a public park. It belongs to everyone now. Perhaps that's just how it should be.

An Inner City Extra

Alang Sauchie, doon Buchie,
alang Argyle tae the Tron,
Up the High tae the Duke an' then
tae the Square anon...

Mine is that undisturbed silence of the heart
which is perfect eloquence.

WILLIAM HAZLITT

THE CLASSIC DEFINITION of any city anywhere is that it contains a cathedral, a university and a market-place. Glasgow is well-qualified on all three elements for city status despite the fact that as I have pointed out earlier, it has technically become a District, the city being the hub-centre of what is now termed Greater Glasgow, the setting for no less than 90 parks. This extra chapter might therefore be considered a bricks and mortar post-script to the nominal 12-parks tour just completed. I still wish I had gone to King's Park, for instance, and at least seen Aikenhead Park – or the lovely Linn with its Snuffmill Bridge, but it's pointless to regret any omissions at this stage. A dozen locations were sufficient for what I had to say in these personal essays.

This inner city addition to this book is only given to offer a glimpse of the contemporary Glasgow and, more importantly, to acknowledge the place of George Square at the very heart of the city centre and, historically, as a park in its own right. As indeed, the records of the current City Council will show. It is fact part of the city's park plan and is therefore a legitimate park exploration for the purposes of this book.

The site was originally marked out in 1871 as an amenity to serve the newly-opened Queen Street railway station but then, in 1881, it became part of a Georgian architectural grid to utilise land to the east and west for civic buildings of quality in order to promote the emerging Glasgow as a city of style and commercial importance. It was recognised by the Victorians that while Glasgow Cross was the historical centre of the town virtually from the time of its first prosperity in the early 18th century, George Square better served the needs of those Glasgow interests who had moved uptown. The square has been strongly tied to Glasgow's history ever since. Yet, for all its Victorian atmosphere, even today, one has to remember that this neat enclosure, this populated and always busy arena, was once a muddy pool filled with dirty water and used mainly for slaughtering horses.

Everything that matters in Glasgow affairs appears to emanate from George Square so we will aim to finish there once we explore its immediate radius known to everyone as the Inner City. The recent International Walkway organised by the City started from the Main door of the City Chambers, but if we are to take the old rhyme noted above as our guide we shall start the city walk further west at *Sauchie*. Sauchiehall Street, as it is properly called is, arguably, the most famous street in the town, so wherever you are in Glasgow, go first to Kelvingrove Art Gallery.

Stand outside its main entrance on Dumbarton Road, turn to the left, and look at what is now the left fork of the road ahead and you are looking at the start of Sauchiehall St. Start walking in the direction of the City Centre. Cross Kelvin Way, walking past the bowling greens and the tennis courts and you are on an urban stroll that will let you see, above shop level, some of the finest domestic and commercial architecture in Britain. Victoria and Edwardian shyly peek out from above and behind the countless coffee-houses and gift shops in street after street. The trick is to keep looking up. The quality is always on the second floor. It's the real thing because it was built *with* money, not to make it. All over the city the architecture rewards the walker with a genuine beauty of line and stone against the sky. This is the old Glasgow in her Sunday best on every day of the week, built before the demands of the motor-car wreaked havoc among stately road-ways and elegant squares and changed the faces of most cities in Britain forever. Glasgow has been through many architectural cycles in its long centuries and coped with every possible change of urban fashion, and it will also weather the effects of '60s municipal short-sightedness and return to its prime.

The first thing that strikes the visitor to Glasgow is the number of churches there are to be seen as your feet carry you towards Charing Cross and the City Centre. Not all are still worshipful places, however, and most have more utilitarian uses these days. Some are theatres, some are furniture stores, some are converted into apartments – an appropriate 'conversion' one would think, although not one that St Mungo might have expected, but they are still splendid buildings and most of their spires still point skywards. Indeed, as has been said, I would hazard that there are as many church spires in Glasgow as there are in Oxford, and it has two more universities, not to mention an iconic Art School and an internationally-recognised Conservatoire of Drama. All of which can be seen in this preliminary canter on the march towards George Square via Charing Cross.

At Charing Cross there is the alternative of crossing through the maze of traffic lights directly on to Sauchiehall or coming onto the Cross via Newton Place and crossing via a particularly ugly pedestrian bridge which is the remnant of an aborted motorway plan for Charing Cross which also left an unfinished road bridge on the southern edge now supporting yet another office building. However, the pedestrian bridge does give a superb viewpoint from which to see the classic red stone tenements surrounding the area and the sight of distant hills all round. Glasgow sits in a basin of hills with the Kilpatrick Hills to the west, the Campsies to the North and East and the Cathkin Braes to the south with the Clyde below leading out to the Irish Sea. It is quite exhilarating to see all this from the centre of a city. Glasgow horizons can be pleasantly surprising.

Descending into Renfrew Street we take the incline up to Garnet Street, turning left into Hill St and continue left until it leads us to the Tenement House Viewpoint and yet another opportunity to take in the view and get your breath back. And if you bow your head you can also take in the poems carved on the paving stones at your feet. Coming out of the Viewpoint, I retraced my steps east along Hill Street, passing the St Aloysius College buildings until we come to Dalhousie and turn right to come on to Renfrew Street, where at No 167 stands one of the most admired buildings in Britain, the Glasgow School of Art. Designed by Glaswegian, Charles Rennie Mackintosh, in 1897 and completed in 1899. It was damaged by fire last year but is already well in the way to be fully restored. This superb facade is now reflected in a more recent construction; an Art School extension whose light green walls are in striking contract to the Mackintosh masterpiece. This is how today looks on yesterday and no doubt tomorrow will see it all from yet another angle. It is what is called progress.

Going downhill from any street we return to Sauchiehall Street and a notice telling me that I am standing at the exact topographical centre of the city. Continuing east among the crowds of shoppers and past the microphones of the various buskers I make my way through the melee of shouts and greetings, bursts of song mixed with laughter and the whole cacophony of city sounds that is Sauchiehall Street on any normal day. Progress down this canal of shops and galleries and coffee tables on the pavement can often be slow but it is made even if there is only a matter of ten paces between shops. I arrive eventually at the steps of the Buchanan Arcade and it is time to take a rest again. There is no better respite than to sit in the sun on stone steps.

I am now within sight of *Buckie*, in other words, Buchanan Street, and the next stage going south. As I walk down past the Subway Station and the old Athenaeum to cross at St Vincent Place I am immediately aware of walking briskly out of the contemporary world and into the faded grandeur of other days where the haughty buildings on either side still look down with some disdain on all below. This is that other Glasgow, the sandstone face that the city used to present to the world, trying its best to survive and having now to live with the pulsating public arena that it has become. Every colour of face is seen here, walking down Buckie, every variation of fashion, every size and shape of person with any sense of posture or pretence. Beauty and bathos meld with ease, for this is *homo sapiens* out for a good time among the bustle and nobody gives a button because nobody has any status in the city throng as dense as this. We can only be ourselves.

Whatever our height, weight, ear-size or nose, we can't help but be part of that great body, that one common entity – *US*! We can disguise ourselves as we like, but we are always the being beneath the wardrobe. We *are* the crowd.

It is noisy here, but it is also exciting, despite the whole broadcasting system of buskers who either scream into microphones or mumble soundlessly. Why don't they just *sing*? Although I do admit I once heard a tenor sing an operatic aria with great effect in this very street and occasionally an old immigrant lady can be seen strumming her guitar and singing a simple song sweetly in a language of her own. It's all part of the continuing cabaret of the streets. Indeed, the whole world mix can be seen in these streets at any one time but, of course, the basic tone is Scottish, even if it has a strong Glasgow overtone. The mandatory bagpiper is usually here, often accompanied by drums. They certainly let go with a heartening swagger.

And then forward, in a flourish that carries us down to the celebrated Princes Square and all that it has to offer the good coffee hunter. I came out restored and continued left towards a view of St Enoch Station, which tells me I am almost at the end of what they call 'The Style Mile'. This label is reinforced by the sight of a top hat standing before a doorway. This gentleman indicates that the Argyle Arcade is ready to usher everyone into a silver covered way glistening with rings, watches and baubles of every kind in a quality shopping avenue that takes us on the next phase – *Argyle*.

Argyle Street is sheer utility enclosed in a long line of big box buildings staring down from windows that tell us nothing about their interiors, and on the pavement before them, black-robed ladies sitting holding empty coffee cups, and saying 'Hi!' to every passer-by. No great crowds here but the road is jammed with traffic – cars, buses, taxis, vans and lorries. A congestion of transportation and no place for the walker. It is wise to come a little off course here and go left up Miller Street for a glimpse of the Modern Arts Museum and the sight of the Duke of Wellington sitting on his horse with a traffic cone on his head. Nobody ever thinks of removing it. It has become one of the Glasgow sights. I was now in Ingram Street, in the heart of what is termed the Merchant City that enclave of restaurants and art shops surrounding the Concert Hall and the Old Fruit Market in Candleriggs.

This is the setting for the annual Merchant City Festival of the arts, which, like the St Mungo's Festival in January is now a regular part of Glasgow cultural life. It can't help but look Bohemian as it brings me forward to the final stage of my town walkabout at the *Tron* at the Trongate, where one used to pay a fee to enter old, medieval Glasgow. Still standing and still wearing its old clothes from centuries ago.

I stand in the *High*, in the ancient High Street under the shadow of the Tolbooth which still towers at the left reminding us that Glasgow goes much further back than Queen Victoria. I move up High Street towards Duke Street with the growing feeling I'm in a different kind of city, all cobbles and grey stone.

Duke Street stands at the site of Glasgow's original university, sited here in the Middle Ages. This faces George Street across High Street and is reputed to be the longest street in Britain but, fortunately, it is not on my schedule today. It starts from The High Street and goes all the way east via Belgrove, Dennistoun, Camlachie, Carntyne, taking in The Forge Retail Park *en route*. (Not our kind of park, I'm afraid. Another misuse of a lovely word.) Duke Street continues all the way up to Parkhead Cross where I stood for so many youthful hours under the clock. But my watch today reminds me that I am due to move west at this point, not east, so I turn left towards George Square, which is ten minutes away, and am glad to take a seat on the first vacant bench and have a final look around before calling it a day.

It is still the palatial City Chambers that dominates the square even without a glimpse of its magnificent marble interior. It was conceived and erected on the east side to set the standard for all the later buildings to rise grandly around the square's concrete borders. An immediate counterpoint was the Merchants' Building on the western side with its splendid dome and unashamed assertion of wealth and status won by the traders and entrepreneurs who did their deals in unashamed Glasgow accents. A hotel was set up on the corner of the north side and to the south the General Post Office headquarters closed the Square with any in-fills being occupied by offices of similar calibre.

Altogether it was an imposing site and it only remained to fill its interior space and in Victorian times, the answer was statues. The first was a pairing to acknowledge Queen Victoria and her consort, Prince Albert, but pride of place in the centre was given to the then celebrity name of the day, Sir Walter Scott, the Borders lawyer turned romantic novelist whose books sold all over Europe in the mid-18th century. I believe he only visited Glasgow once, yet this was the first ever monument to be erected given to Scott, an even earlier compliment than his Edinburgh memorial.

Other statues follow around the edges with the famous names of their day: soldiers, politicians, inventors, and one poet, Robert Burns of course, who was built later by public demand. The only really meaningful monument is the Memorial to the Dead of Two World Wars erected with money from the Earl Haig Fund. The sad irony is that the same General Haig led so many to their death in the trenches of First World War.

Army tanks were the feature of one rally in the Square in 1919 when thousands rallied here to protest about poor pay and working conditions in the year after the end of that same war. 'Bloody Friday' as it was called, had been organised by the new Socialist pioneers known as the Red Clydesiders, many of whom were jailed in Edinburgh for their political pains.

Down the years there were many more such spontaneous rallies and demonstrations in the Square, the most atypical being that which occurred to mark the death of Mrs Thatcher, the controversial Prime Minister of Great Britain and the *bete-noire* of all Trade Unionists. In contrast, and to offset unrest, the Council imposed conditions for the use of the Square for public gatherings and green lawns were created at each corner and benches provided so that passing citizens might take advantage of them to find a moment of ease and gossip, even a time for contemplation away from the noise and the traffic in the surrounding streets. Another irony is that this very question has arisen again in the city as opposition councillors have on this very day, as I write this, moved that commercial events be relocated from the city centre to more appropriate sites so that 'The Square be restored to the people for purposes of congregation, meetings and relaxation.' This would exactly fulfil its original purpose and it's to be hoped that it will duly come to pass.

The space does look a little tired and it does need an inspired reawakening. Various schemes have been put forward in recent years but none has come to fruition for all kinds of reasons, including a stubborn unwillingness to change, high costs and sheer inefficiency, not quite the hallmarks of the Glaswegians who made the town what it was once. It became the Second City of the Empire because these Victorian citizens had courage, optimism and most of all, imagination and vision. Qualities still needed today if George Square is to come into its own again.

Speaking personally, I would like to see all the statuary removed, and resited to present-day pedestrian thoroughfares such as Sauchiehall Street or Buchanan Street. Studded through the centre of these streets they would be further attractions and more appreciated especially if seats were added at the bases to provide welcome rests. In George Square itself trees could be planted again. This would be in keeping with its recreational aim and greatly assist its visual appeal. George Square is the real hub of Glasgow; people resort to it as they do to Trafalgar Square in London. Ordinary people can make their voices heard here even if it's only at new year. The Square is always 'there' for Glaswegians, and will be what modern make-up it applies to its weathered old face. As the well-known slogan states: 'PEOPLE MAKE GLASGOW' which is why, in the older slogan, we were told that 'Glasgow Smiles Better!'

All this came to back to me again as I sat on bench taking it all in. I thought of all the walking I had done in the last month around my chosen parks. Now the job was to put it all down on paper. As I glanced over my shoulder at the wonderful facade of the City Chambers I thought of the huge presumption it was for a city in mid-Victorian times to spend more than half-million pounds, an immense sum then, on offices for clerks and talkers. But it has more than paid for itself in the respect it has won as an image of Glasgow, and deservedly so.

Very soon, a new frontage is to go up on the hotel by the Queen Street Railway Station. It will look over the entire Square, but more importantly, those in the Square then will look up at its ultra-modern face and see the 22nd century beckoning...

Conclusion

That Glasgow, on the base of commerce rose
A noble fabric, all the world knows.

ANONYMOUS 1773; GLASGOW MUSEUM

THE FACT IS Glasgow did indeed rise, and what I learned first from these 12 park walks was that the dear, green part of the city was and will continue to be a big part of that growth. It proffers a component that was not only useful to city life, but beautiful in its totality and it is this beauty that is its greatest asset, if only for what it adds to the human environment. I sensed this more and more as I followed my own rather than the many designated routes. I relied on the whim of the moment in many instances so that I might get a sense of actuality and reality in that living, spontaneous moment.

This often led me a little astray at times, I admit, but in most cases, wherever I walked, it was nearly always enjoyable. Except, of course, when I was imprisoned in that thorn bush or soaked with rain. Whatever the weather or the mood that I was in, or the state of my toes, I was always open to the constant surprises encountered, to the many visual delights met with on the way, which were infinitely more than I ever expected. Even more so for the people I met *en route*. They were characters all of them and I know I got round all the easier because of them. I was constantly taken aback by their kindness, worldly knowledge and originality, but most of all, by their Glasgow sense of humour. 'You've got to laugh' is an imperative on both banks of the Clyde.

Billy Connolly, a Glasgow man of well-deserved worldwide fame, once said of his native city:

The time for trumpet-blowing and naive pleas for recognition is long gone. If you are lucky enough to have been born there, or smart enough to want to live there, then the time has come to be quietly pleased.

Of course, Billy now lives in New York! Yet the truth is Billy has never really left Glasgow because it is always in him, and will always be. As it will with me. Like Billy I have gone all over the world with the job I had as a working actor. I merely followed where it led me and it led me back to Glasgow. If my friend Billy has similarly landed up in the United States, good luck to him.

I know his heart, like mine, will have its permanent billet in Glasgow. Both of us have Glasgow in our systems. Its industrial fumes have indelibly stained our voices, its street noises were our first music and its green parks released our visual imagination. Glasgow still belongs to us. We can't part with it, because we *are* still part of it.

I realise this even more now that I've made my own park selection. My parks only scratch the surface of what Glasgow has to offer, but I'm happy to have made my journey, however modest, even if only for the variety and diversity discovered. Not one of the parks is like any other and that is their first virtue. The parks are mirrors. They reflect their city and help us, from season to season, to see it in many different lights, so many colours, so many shades of green. Like Charles Rennie Mackintosh, who wrote of his own painting, 'I see green in everything...' By seeing Glasgow in my green fashion I have at the same time, have seen my fellow citizens in a new light. Not as part of the park landscape or as the chorus found in the theatricality of the streets but in the way they are seen as living organisms themselves, of every kind and colour.

We ourselves are growing things, not only in Glasgow, but everywhere. And everywhere means people, ordinary people in the universal park that is our present complicated and misdirected world. As we grow we are all capable of flowering naturally if we would only leave it to nature instead of to society. After all, climate change and other environmental hazards are our own doing, not anyone else's. If the whole world came from nothing then obviously, at some stage, it will return to nothing. That's the way of all created matter, but we needn't hurry it along. We can delay things by living cleaner lives, in the wholly natural sense and not get tied up in the temporary plastic norm.

The green crusade ought to be our first priority because it's more than cutting carbon emissions, burying plastic or burning the increasing amount of rubbish. It's doing what the Woodland Trust does, it's planting seeds and growing trees wherever a space appears, it's giving back fresh air to the modern world. It's giving people space to breathe in our crazy over-active world. It's in persuading everyone to rise up and move around in areas other than supermarkets, coffee shops and car-parks. Parking should have a new, fresh meaning and it would have nothing to do with cars. I have a fancy that one night I would get up and, brush and paint-pot in hand, go round Glasgow painting out the 'N' of 'No Parking' and replacing it with a 'G' so that all those signs would read: 'GO PARKING'. That would soon wake people up. At least it provides a working slogan.

As soon as the first humans fell from the trees they had to walk in order to find food. They became nomadic and the earth, as we know it, opened up to them. Our forefathers had no alternative but to walk everywhere, to act according to exterior conditions. The interior life was an undiscovered country to them although there was a simmering of the aesthetic and the spiritual there as cave drawings show. The instinct to walk and explore is still in us all today wherever we live in the world. Scientists now tell us that our globe is now entering its sixth 'extinction', due to the 'toxic mix' of habitat destruction. Add oceanic acidification and the climate could soon become as malodorous as that which wiped out the dinosaurs 65 million years ago following a catastrophic, natural event. But our catastrophic event will be self-inflicted.

The contemporary idea of parks for people has more than a local intent. The United States has its Trust for Public Land working on the principle that everyone has a right to access to a green space for play and recreation. The meaning of the very word 'recreation' is, after all, to re-create. To begin again, to make a fresh start. How welcome that is in most lives, a second chance. Apparently, ten million Americans live no further than ten minutes from a park. Greater Glasgow's less than two million inhabitants have parks all about them and they are well used. Parks connect people to each other and to themselves.

Yet it takes effort to lean forward and look closely, to become involved, and even more to get up and do something. We are not vegetables, we are organisms. That means we are still animals, but animals with brains, active feelings and a soul. These are attributes underused by most of us – at least in trio. Small wonder they deteriorate. They have to be used, and used well to be to be of value. The more they are walked over, the better they will be looked after, for good use makes for good care and caring is only another word for love.

The surrounding universe will do its thing in its own time whatever we decide. Our own time is limited, not by stamina, but by the natural order of things, therefore the worst thing in the world is to waste it. The passing years go by, but we ourselves are deteriorating by the hour as we age, so it only makes sense to try to live by the moment. That's the secret. If you have good reason to get up in the morning and show a reluctance to retire to bed at night, you have no reason to complain. Seize the day indeed and make it work for you instead of trapping you in its mounting inessentials. Know what you want to do and do it.

Know Thyself first is perhaps the oldest advice given in the world but we would all enjoy that world a lot more if we just give to what we find about us instead of surrendering to the false promises of high finance and the sheer lie of celebrity. We must wrest the world away from the political talkers and get back to the natural simplicity of living as we find it.

The young generation is being totally mislead by its insistent pre-occupation with social media. What's social about keeping your head down and hardly seeing where you are going? They are being misled by the little picture box they hold in their hands, with its tyrannical line to their ears. They should be looking up and about, seeing other people and other realities. This is a natural stimulus that is undermined by the fashion worldwide for appliances instead of being stimulated by living and breathing actuality. Above all perhaps, they should get some fresh air, get out into the open more, take a walk in the park. It will at least open their eyes to alternative visions and sounds other than their own. Safe in a unified and cohesive environment that is that is the park the walker is free to resort to a totally natural physical rhythm. Rhythm is good, because it is stimulating and often comforting. And when we can't walk any further, then the only thing to do is to sit down somewhere and be QUIET.

Quiet, or peace or silence whichever name one applies to it, is surely the last true luxury left to us today. Noise of every kind is a concomitant of living as far as I can tell, and the whisper has almost been forgotten. Bring back peace and quiet is my cry now, and if it isn't to be found, then create, or re-create it, is and where you can whatever the weather or personal circumstances. Calm is an under-rated commodity but it is entirely an interior off-shoot of exterior silence. Make one and the other comes as a bonus. It has a medical benefit, a moral uplift and a welcome change from whatever is the pattern of living for anyone. Above all else it offers calm and that's what everyone needs at the difficult times, to know how to KEEP CALM.

Music helps and the ear-phone could come into its own on park walks. The type of music wouldn't matter. Anything from Elgar to Elvis would do but something soft and smooth would be a lovely companion to a leisurely stroll in a green land.

The mention of Elgar reminds me that for a time he was band-master at the Worcester Asylum and worked with one of the staff there, a Dr Sherlock, who specialised in music therapy for his disturbed patients and Elgar wrote pieces exactly for this purpose. This developed into his later style which produced 'Salut d'Amour' for instance which was exactly the sort of thing I wanted to hear in my ear as I moved through the park. I did try it tentatively but I soon gave it up because, personally, I found my attention was divided from what I was seeing and what I was hearing.

Every park has a voice of its own and one has to pay close attention in order to hear it – because park music does not come from earphones or the bandstand nor from the birds – but in no noise at all, from *absolute silence*. Many of the best moments I experienced on the walks was the value of silence and its companion, stillness and how rare both virtues are. It's difficult to upset anyone when you are still or to offend when you are silent. I found in the open air that when these two conditions applied I was in another space and I loved it because I *lived* it. Hamish Fulton must have felt something of the same when, in 1988, he walked for seven days through the Cairngorms in the Highlands of Scotland seeking silence. No talking for a week? What a test that that must have been but what a joy to have done it. I'd love to see a place, other than a church, of course, that assured me of real silence. Perhaps the first step would be to create a green space in ourselves, an innate sense of the exterior in the interior as it were. After all, wise minds tell us we ought to cultivate a quiet centre in ourselves if only as a point of reference when the outside world is unusually invasive.

This is what gave me the idea of the Quiet House. If I had my way I would have one in every park. It would be a modest construction, no more than a small timber overhang with a seat, but it would provide a shelter, a space where talking or singing or the playing of music is strictly forbidden and total silence prevails. No notices art works or murals should be on display except the one injunction: SILENCE PLEASE. In such an environment, with the park all around it, the individual would be free to be alone with his or her thoughts and emotions, either physical or spiritual – no one's business but their own. What a haven the quiet house would be. Or should I say heaven?

Unfortunately, in today's cultural climate, such a cabin might well be four round narrow poles with a canvas covering and a notice saying: 'Bring your own chair'. Anything, I suppose, to avoid the graffiti fiends and the inveterate carvers and initialisers. Pity.

Meantime, we must enjoy what we can, endure what we have to and trust that our walk through life will be as rewarding and uplifting in the end as the best walk we ever had through a park. Given the will and the way, falling back on all their innate qualities of cheerful acceptance and natural *brio* the Glaswegians will make sure their city remains great. They have only to trust in the energy, good-will, imagination and good sense that have brought them from a trickle on the hill to a mighty river that runs all the way to the sea; from a wood and straw hut to a cathedral; from a swampy wasteland to a crown of magnificent parks, each a jewel of its own making and proud to show it.

Altogether, the Glasgow story is a wonderful adventure of attainment, excitement, triumph and disaster with a sturdy application to survival no matter the odds. It has bred a tough skin but sensitive hearts and its parks are further proof of this. It shows that as people, one way or another, we have to find our way back to a simpler world and perhaps the best way to do that is to do more and say less. Whoever we think we are at this moment, and wherever we think we are supposed to be going, we are all, at root, the same. Because, essentially, we are all heading the same way. Why not enjoy the company of our fellow-travellers while we can?

The old Irish saying has it, 'In the shadow of our friends, we grow'. That's so true, friends are to be cherished. Remember, old friends are gold. We don't inherit them like family, we make them by accident, by incident, by and way of casual or mutual interest. This contact that is part of our social instinct, but it is only with a few that the contact adheres and grows into the auxiliary love that is true friendship. Yes, real friendship is to be cherished. If you open to it, it will come your way, however unexpectedly. Even while walking in a park, especially a Glasgow park. Just like its people, Glasgow enjoys a good chat, and that's what a good park does, it makes a conversation with you. So keep your ears open as well as your eyes. It will be worth it.

My Glasgow today is much more than a working-class city. There is a very rich and comfortable middle-class citizenship living here today who can mince words with the best, an educated layer that can cope with the highest level of debate, also a modern artistic and musical population with an international reputation, a leadership that still has vision. Last year, because of blight and decay in certain areas, Glasgow City Council put forward a £400,000 plan in association with the local councils within the Clyde Valley area, to implement infrastructure projects that will take run-down areas, such as the Clyde waterfront, the Collegelands, the old Calton Barras and the Forth and Clyde Canal at the City Centre, and designated sites in North Glasgow on to a new level over the next decade.

This City Deal, as it is called, is in the same spirit of regeneration and far-sightedness that prompted the early-Victorian city fathers, and their immediate successors, to create Glasgow's unique heritage of parks and recreation grounds. It is done now, as it was then, not only to transform the economy but to give Glasgow and the Clyde Valley further amenities and places of beauty with a metropolitan framework. The lessons of the past have been learned, decor means as much as drainage, and the image of Glasgow and its growing international status will continue to improve in the years to come. We who live here will work to keep alive that spirit that fed our forebearers and made us what we are, Glaswegians.

Yes, Glasgow *will* flourish. One day that bell *will* ring, the tree *will* grow, the fish *will* swim and the bird *will* fly over the dear, green place that is yet to come...

This little bit of my own *Glescapeak* says it all:

We came in heid furst an' we gang oot feet furst.
An' whit we ur, is in atween.
But then anon, gin an 'oor is gawn,
It's as if we've never been.
We're birthed, we learn, an' then we earn,
We buy the richt tae be,
We eat, we drink, we sleep, we think,
We dream, an' then we dee.

That's it in a nutshell – a Glasgow nutshell. There's no need to say more.

Appendix

OTHER CURRENT District Council Parks and Leisure Spaces in Glasgow City:

Auldhouse Park; Barlanark Park; Cardonald Park; Castlemilk Park; Cathkin Braes Park; Cowlairs Park; Cranhill Park; Croftcroighn Park; Cross Park; Darnley Mill Park; Dawsholm Park; Dowanhill Park; Drumchapel Park; Elder Park; Glenconnor Park; Govanhill Park; Greenfield Park; King's Park; Knightswood Park; Linn Park; Lochair Park; Lochlomond Park; Maryhill Park; Maxwell Park; Milton Park; Newlands Park; Plantation Park; Pollokshaws Park; Possil Park; Richmond Park; Rosshall Park; Ruchill Park; Rutherglen Park; Titwood Park; Toryglen Park; Westhorn Park.

Also Recreation Grounds at:

Barlia Drive; Dalmarnock; Gorbals Rest; Helenvale Sports; Holmlea; King George's Field; Langland's Road; Lister Street; Newfield Square: Househill; Penilee; Petershill: Smeaten Street; South Pollok; Temple Yoker and Yorkhill. As I complete this book, Fields in Trust have launched a nation-wide search to find the best park in the UK, and the people of Glasgow have been asked to nominate their own choice of park for an annual award, and communities across the whole country are being asked to name their favourite park, recreation ground or green space. So it would appear that parks are back in fashion.

In addition, a recent study at the London School of Economics has declared:

'Given the obesity epidemic, and given that a large proportion of people in the UK are inactive, recommending that people walk briskly more often is a cheap and easy policy option.' In other words, a walk in the park is better than a work-out.

Just what I've been trying to say!

There have been feelings in these walks that gave me moments of nothing less than awe in seeing something awesome, in being provoked to deeper thought and above all in being made to feel grateful for life. I gather that awe can now be added to the medicine chest in that, according to scientists in Stanford California, 'a small dose of awe can give a boost of life satisfaction. In other words, as I have tried to convey previously, awe is healthy. Awe therapy, even in small doses, is good for you and it's available – free – in any park near you.

Acknowledgements

My sincere thanks are due to:

The Right Honourable, the Lord Provost of Glasgow, Lord Lieutenant, Sadie Docherty; Gavin MacDougall of Luath Press, whose idea this book was, and his editing team, especially Lotte Mitchell Reford, who worked so efficiently on it, and Hilary Bell and Juliette King. Also to Staff at the Special Collections at the Mitchell Library in North Street, Glasgow for detailed research; Sarah Keegan, Glasgow City Council Receptionist for starting me off on the walks; Sean Cochrane, Glasgow Council Contacts, for action advice; Alanna Knight, Ray Neale and John O'Leary for encouraging comments; Frank McKain for his letter to the press; and to the many Glasgow individual characters who helped with the narrative along the way, too many to name individually but each of them appreciated. Also friends like Dame Katharine Liston for her eagle eye; Graham Roxburgh for information on his House for an Art Lover; Anne Ross for the same on Glasgow trees; Jim Friel and Willie Gallacher for Glasgow memories, also Jim Stoddart in 'The Scottish Banner' for likewise; and to all the city bus drivers, taxi drivers, train drivers, and to various friends and family for getting me to the parks on time but who often happily left me to get back home on my own!

Lastly, to all those strangers in the park who passed me on the many paths I walked and never failed to give me a smile, a grin, a nod, a 'Good Morning' or 'Fine day' or even 'Terrible weather, is it no'?' and the park staff everywhere who couldn't have been more helpful or more proud of the job they did. It made the research for this volume a joy and the writing of it a sincere tribute to them all.

Suggested Further Reading

A Parochial View of Glasgow – Alfred Forbes Smith, A&A Enterprises,
Scotland 1997

A Glasgow Man's Tuppence Worth – Alfred Forbes Smith, Clydeside
Press, Glasgow 2010

A World Tour of My Glasgow – Alfred Forbes, Clydeside Press,
Glasgow 2006

Auld Hawkie and Others... Dorothy Whitaker, Glasgow District
Libraries, 1988

Barrapatter – Elspeth King (Editor) People's Palace Print 1983–85

Building the Dream – Graham Roxburgh – Roxburgh Publications,
Glasgow 2006

City of Glasgow, The – Photographs by Colin Baxter, Lomond Books,
Edinburgh 1994

East End to West End – John Cairney, Mainstream Publishing,
Edinburgh 1988

Echoes from a Glasgow Tenement – Alfred Forbes Smith, Clydeside
Press, Glasgow 2001

Empire Exhibition of Glasgow – Bob Crampsey, Mainstream Publishing,
Edinburgh 1988

Glasgow – A Celebration – Edited by Cliff Hanley, Mainstream
Publishing, Edinburgh 1984

Glasgow – David Daiches, Andre Deutsch, London 1977

Glasgow – Ian Archer/Douglas Corrance, Mainstream Publishing,
Edinburgh 1988

Glasgow – Irene Maver, Edinburgh University Press, 2000

Glasgow As It Was (3vols) – Michael Moss/John Hume, Hendon
Publishing, Nelson 1975

Glasgow at War 1939–45 – Paul Harris, Archive Productons, Glasgow
1986

Glasgow by the way, but – John Cairney, Luath Press, Edinburgh
2006/07

Glasgow Encyclopedia, The – Joe Fisher, Mainstream Publishing,
Edinburgh 1994

Glasgow in your Pocket – Collins Pocket Maps

Glasgow – Fabric of a City – Maurice Lindsay, Robert Hale, London
2001

Glasgow Herald Book of Glasgow – introduction by Arnold Kemp,
Glasgow 1989

Glasgow's Miles Better – John Struthers, Struthers Advertising &
Marketing, Glasgow 1986

Glasgow Paintings – Anthony Armstrong, Glasgow Collections,
Glasgow 1990

Glasgow Public Parks – Edited by 'Noremac', Cameron Publishing, Glasgow 1908

Glasgow Public Park, The – Duncan McLellan, John Smith & Son, Glasgow 1894

Glasgow Scene Again – Alfred Forbes Smith, A&A Enterprises, Scotland 1998

Glasgow Smile, The – Alan Brown, Birlinn Ltd, Edinburgh 2013

Glasgow Story, The – Colm Brogan, Frederick Muller, London 1952

Glasgow Street Atlas, Harper-Collins, London 2002

Glasgow – The First 800 Years – Hugh Cochrane, City of Glasgow Council, circa 1975

Glasgow,40 Town and Country Walks – John Craig/Katie Smith, Pocket Mountains Ltd 2008

Great Glasgow Stories – John Burrowes, Mainstream Publishing, Edinburgh 1998

I Belong to Glasgow – Alfred Forbes Smith, Clydeside Press, Glasgow 2000

Leisure in the Parks – Official Programme 1965 – Corporation of Glasgow.

Look Up Glasgow – Adrian Searle/ David Barbour, Freight Books, Glasgow 2013

No Mean City – H. Kingsley-Long and Alexander McArthur, Corgi Books, Glasgow 1935

Our Glasgow – Piers Dudgeon, Headline Review, London 2009

Pilgrim Guide to Scotland – Dr Donald Smith, Saint Andrew's Press, Edinburgh 2015

Played in Glasgow – Ged O'Brien, Heritage Scotland and Glasgow City Council 2004

Queen's Park – Ian Marshall and Ronald Smith, Glasgow City Council, 1997

Quest for Charles Rennie Mackintosh, The – John Cairney, Luath Press, Edinburgh 2004

Strathclyde – Photographs by Douglas Corrance, Collins, Glasgow 1985

The Patter – Michael Munro, Glasgow District Libraries, 1986 and 1988

This City Now – Ian R Mitchell, Luath Press, Edinburgh 2005

Trees of Glasgow – John Miller, Dingwall Printers, Dingwall 2005

Walking Though Glasgow's Industrial Past – Ian R Mitchell, Luath Press, Edinburgh 2015

All Glasgow newspapers of the time and Glasgow City Council Heritage Brochures and all leaflets on City Parks

Some other books published by **LUATH** PRESS

Glasgow by the way, but: Celebrating a City

John Cairney

ISBN: 978-1-906307-10-3 PBK £7.99

 Do you love going to the pictures? Live for the season's Old Firm match? Have a 'rerr' singer in the family? Long to dance under the stars in the Barras ballroom? Is your idea of a local hero Lobby Dosser? And who needs Bob Dylan when you have Matt McGinn?

In this carefully constructed homage, John Cairney takes you on a tour of his Glasgow, introducing the people and places that have shaped it. Full of the humour, tension and patter that defines Scotland's most charismatic city, everyone will be sure to find a part of their own Glasgow reflected in Cairney's honest evocation of his home city. *Glasgow by the way, but* is the written tribute Glasgow has been waiting for, from one of its most famous sons.

A good read, even to venerable Edinburghers.
EVENING TIMES

The Quest for Charles Rennie Mackintosh

John Cairney

ISBN: 978-1-905222-43-8 PBK £8.99

 Charles Rennie Mackintosh is established in the Scottish iconography as an architect of originality, a designer of genius and a painter of exceptional quality. He is, however, an enigma as a man.

For the last thirty years John Cairney has been on a personal quest to find the complex man behind the façade that was Charles Rennie Mackintosh, architect and artist. Though recognised even in his own day as a genius, he was by no means a saint of high morals and mystic vision. He was a flesh and blood charmer, who attracted women as much as he irritated men. He was all artist, but also all man, with the advantages and disadvantages of both.

This book explores many hitherto unexamined aspects of Toshie's life, delving into the significance of Mackintosh's relationship with his mother, the importance of his first girlfriend, and how much his wife, Margaret Macdonald, contributed to his life. This is the life of an ordinary Glasgow man with extraordinary talent, a great love story with personal complications, professional conflicts, triumphs and disasters, and an engulfing tragic ending.

Details of these and other books published by Luath Press can be found at: **www.luath.co.uk**

Luath Press Limited
committed to publishing well written books worth reading

LUATH PRESS takes its name from Robert Burns, whose little collie Luath (*Ga*
swift or nimble) tripped up Jean Armour at a wedding and gave him the chance
speak to the woman who was to be his wife and the abiding love of his life.
Burns called one of 'The Twa Dogs' Luath after Cuchullin's
hunting dog in Ossian's *Fingal*. Luath Press was established
in 1981 in the heart of Burns country, and now resides
a few steps up the road from Burns' first lodgings on
Edinburgh's Royal Mile.
Luath offers you distinctive writing with a hint of
unexpected pleasures.

Most bookshops in the UK, the US, Canada, Australia,
New Zealand and parts of Europe either carry our books
in stock or can order them for you. To order direct from
us, please send a £sterling cheque, postal order, international
money order or your credit card details (number, address of
cardholder and expiry date) to us at the address below. Please add
post and packing as follows: UK – £1.00 per delivery address; overseas surface mail – £2.50 per delivery address; overseas airmail –
£3.50 for the first book to each delivery address, plus £1.00 for each
additional book by airmail to the same address. If your order is a gift, we will happ
enclose your card or message at no extra charge.

Luath Press Limited
543/2 Castlehill
The Royal Mile
Edinburgh EH1 2ND
Scotland

Telephone: 0131 225 4326 (24 hours)
email: sales@luath.co.uk
Website: www.luath.co.uk